HOW TO MASTER
PRECISION
FLIGHT

BY DAVID A. FRAZIER

TAB BOOKS Inc.
BLUE RIDGE SUMMIT, PA. 17214

Other TAB Books by the Author

No. 2247 *AG Pilot Flight Training Guide – including FAR Part 137*
No. 2290 *The ABC's of Safe Flying*

FIRST EDITION

FIRST PRINTING

Copyright © 1984 by TAB BOOKS Inc.

Printed in the United States of America

Library of Congress Cataloging in Publication Data

Frazier, David, 1944-
     How to master precision flight.

     Includes index.
     1. Airplanes—Piloting. I. Title.
TL710.F75   1984   629.132′521   83-24348
ISBN 0-8306-2354-X (pbk.)

Contents

Acknowledgments

My thanks go out to Jay Wolf, Kevin Frayer, and Blaine Martin for technical assistance and, as always, to Joe Christy for being there whenever I am in trouble. I thank you all sincerely.

To my beloved family: Janene, my wife; Vincent, my son; Vicki, my daughter; and Bandit, my cat, who sat on my desk throughout the entire manuscript. I love you all.

Introduction

Since the dawn of aviation, man has been the weakest link in the aviation chain. Much of this weakness is due to a lack of knowledge and skill in basic flight techniques. Too many pilots are involved in aircraft accidents—or incidents—because they have either not learned, or do not put to use, the firm habit patterns that they must take with them on each and every flight. To put it simply, *they are not precise.*

The files of the FAA and NTSB are full of needless aircraft accidents—accidents that point to a common source, the pilot. And they point even deeper—to sloppy teaching and mechanical learning. These bad habits must not be allowed to continue. Are you one of those pilots who believes that close is good enough? *It's not.* It is imperative that we all master precision flight techniques—you, me, and everyone.

The need for precision is evident in most aspects of daily living. How would you like a carpenter to build you a house with doors and windows that *almost* closed, or a tire dealer to sell you some tires that were *almost* round? Or how would you like to ride in an airplane whose wings *usually* stayed on? Not on your life, right? Well, your life could be the thing at stake if precision isn't taken seriously.

Your goal of becoming a precise pilot must start with your attitude—the way you think. You have to learn to plan ahead and attempt to imagine every possible problem that may crop up on a given flight. You must learn to expect the unexpected and train yourself to act accordingly. If you have been lucky enough to have had a good teacher, and you are smart enough to take the basics you have learned and build from there, then you have a better-than-average chance of becoming a precise pilot. If you had a less-than-enthusiastic instructor or if you have the mistaken notion that all the bad things happen to the other guy, you could be in for some real problems. I have repeatedly told my own students that *a thinking pilot is a safer pilot,* and this I firmly believe for many reasons.

If you are really thinking about what you are doing, then chances are that you are on top of the situation. If, on the other hand, you are reliving last night's love affair or looking forward to what may happen tonight, you are setting yourself up for the possibility of some real surprises—and I don't mean the kind you want to write home about.

Several years ago, we had a very bad ice storm here in the Midwest. The airport at which I teach, as well as everything else, was covered with a layer of ice about a half inch thick. It was so bad that I didn't even go out to the airport for several days. When I finally got to the airport, it was a sight to behold—ice, *everywhere* ice. I even had trouble walking the 20 or 30 feet from my car to the terminal without serious peril to my backside.

As I made my way into the terminal, I saw several other previously housebound instructors standing around talking about the conditions of our 63 acres of ramp, runways, roads, etc. The consensus was that we were all crazy for being there, but since we had nothing better to do, we might as well shoot the bull and take in the beauty of the frozen landscape.

I was leaning in a doorway, talking to our secretary about the sheer beauty of the ice-laden trees, when I heard what sounded like jet engines. For a moment my mind would not believe the sound my ears said they were hearing. Would anyone be so crazy as to even taxi on this 3600-acre skating rink? No, it couldn't be—it must be the furnace, or someone upstairs using a vacuum cleaner. No, it *was* a jet!

I ran to the windows on the east side of the terminal and there it was—a corporate jet, gear and flaps down, nose high, just about to touch down on our one-mile-long runway 18. I remember thinking, "Is he nuts?" Or words to that effect.

In less time than it took to wonder if the pilot was sitting on his brains, he touched down, transforming himself from the captain of a sleek jet into the driver of a 120-knot bobsled on a straight one-mile-long, 150-foot wide course—with little means of slowing his machine. The aircraft was *not* equipped with thrust reversers, as we were soon to discover.

The events of the next 30 or so seconds seemed to be in slow motion. The pilot held the nose off as long as he could, presumably for better aerodynamic braking. When the nose came down, he retracted the flaps and spoilers—then he put them back into the slipstream again. This scene was repeated several times as the jet continued straight on down the runway. The pilot was trying to slow the hurtling aircraft, but too many things were against him.

I felt for him as the jet sped on down the runway. I knew the feeling of the knot that had to be forming in the pit of his stomach—the kind you get when you are in a situation over which you can exercise so little control, along with the inward anger you have at placing yourself in that situation to begin with. I could also visualize his frantic movements in the cockpit as he tried every means at his disposal to halt the aircraft. I could almost hear his thoughts: "Damn, think I'll . . . No! Damn!"

As the jet neared the departure end of the runway, maybe 500 feet from the end, he found a dry patch about 100 feet long and maybe three feet wide. He managed to put his left main landing gear into the dry spot and apply the brakes. The asymmetrical braking action caused the jet to jaw about 90 degrees to the left. It was in this unusual attitude—sideways to the direction of the runway—that the jet plunged off the departure end of the runway, slid about 200 yards into a cornfield, and finally came to rest.

Being over a half mile from the aircraft, we at the terminal could not see if there was any major damage to the jet. As we tried to make our way over the glare ice to the crash and fire trucks, we could see no sign of smoke or fire coming from the scene. In fact, we didn't see or hear anything—no sounds, no perceptible movement, no doors opening, nothing.

Then, just as we were about to enter the trucks, there came the unmistakable sounds of jet engines spooling up. The pilot was apparently going to try to taxi the jet out of the cornfield and back onto the runway. We watched in awe as the jet began to shake and vibrate as the engines wound up tighter and tighter. Then it began to move! This fellow was going to taxi a corporate jet out of a frozen cornfield, through several hundred yards of ice and cornstalks, and back onto the runway. I couldn't believe it.

He taxied the jet—now more icebreaker than aircraft—back to the runway, shut it down and got out to inspect it for damage, and then continued on up and parked it in front of the terminal. Five of the most gray humans I have ever seen got out of the jet and made their way into the terminal building.

Once inside, we asked the pilot what he was thinking about that would make him attempt a landing on an ice-covered runway. His answer was that he thought the runway was wet, but not frozen. We then gave him a little piece of information that shook him right down to his toes. You see, for some reason known but to God, runway 9-27 was *completely dry*. He had an identical, dry one-mile long runway available, but chose instead to land on ice. Why? Because he left out one important piece of precision in an otherwise precise flight: He didn't bother to call in on Unicom and obtain an airport advisory. Had he bothered to call in and inquire, this near tragedy could most certainly have been avoided. (By the way, the aircraft suffered only a broken hydraulic line, which was fixed by a mechanic before the group took off for their destination—on runway 27.)

The point I'm trying to drive home with this tale is that to be a precise pilot you must take into consideration *all* factors at your disposal, known and unknown. You have to practice and learn, watch, listen, and ask if you ever hope to reach that intangible proficiency which the really good pilots seek. You have to think and plan ahead in order to avoid getting yourself into a situation for which you are not ready to cope. In short, real precision will not be thrust upon you; you must work for it.

How often have you heard the old joke, "How do you get to Carnegie Hall? Practice, practice, practice." Well, this is one way of putting it; working your butt off would be closer to the truth. It will take a good deal of dedication and hard work for you to become a really precise pilot. You will have to train yourself to strive for much better proficiency than is required merely to pass a flight test and oral examination. Remember, to pass an FAA oral and flight exam, you only have to meet *minimum* requirements. While it's true that you may be certificated as a pilot by meeting minimum standards, I know of no really precise pilot who does not exceed minimum standards by a wide margin. If you are satisfied with minimum performance, I suggest you sell this book to someone who isn't satisfied with being an average pilot, throw it away, use it to start fires in your fireplace, or anything else you can think of to do with it. But don't read on. Precision can be catching.

Okay, now that we've separated into groups, how do you go about becoming a precision pilot? It starts, like most all worthwhile endeavors, with an individual commitment to rise above the norm, to excel. To do this in aviation you must start at the beginning, with your basic flight technique, and build from there. You must seek knowledge wherever you can find it—from a good instructor, a good book, observation of other piloting techniques, and so on. Good ideas are all around you. All you have to do is sort through and separate the helpful from the harmful, the known from the unknown.

If you are just beginning to learn to fly, you will want to select a flight school with instructors who have a reputation for demanding precision and who consistently turn out really good pilots. Check around. Ask questions of students at a given flight school. See if they are confident about the training they are receiving. If they had to do it all over again, would they choose this same school? The same instructor? If the answer is yes, you have probably found a pretty good place to begin your training. If, on the other hand, the general atmosphere is one of dismay or unhappiness, you had better look further. Don't take the word of just one student. Get an overall feel. You may run into someone who has just failed a phase check and is bitter at the instructor when the real blame may lie with the student himself. In this case, you probably won't obtain a true picture of that flight school.

If you already are a certificated pilot, you may still have some questions about your ability to fly with precision. If you have such questions, the chances are good that these doubts in themselves should be telling you something. You most likely need some meaningful dual from a good instructor to shore up your skill level. Notice I said *meaningful* dual. Don't just pay someone to ride with you to admire the scenery. This happens all too often, especially when the pilot has acquired some flight time, and the instructor might feel that if you're still alive after this long, why bother? If you run into an instructor with this opinion, lose him—*fast*.

In the final analysis, it is up to *you* to decide which path to take—precise or average. Precision will involve a great deal more effort on your part. You will have to make a concerted effort to learn as much as possible about a given task or maneuver. You will have to look at "average" as something not in your vocabulary. "Average" will have to become only the point at which you start on your road of surpassing minimum flight qualifications.

You will have to learn to pace your learning in order to glean the most from your experience level. Don't expect to become a precision pilot from the very first time you try a given task. *Do*, however, expect nothing short of precision as your ultimate goal. This is the important thing: to continue to strive for perfection, for since there is no such thing as perfection, you can only get better and better. You can only learn more and more about your own coordination, skill, thinking ability, and level of competence. You will gain an insight into both the workings of flight and of your own mental and physical capabilities. Go for it. Be the best.

In the following chapters, I will look at flight from the earliest stages of training through the more complex maneuvers. I will start at the beginning and build. This is exactly how your training must proceed—from the foundation to the complete pilot. You will have to remember there are no shortcuts to becoming a truly precise pilot. You have to start at the bottom, lay a firm foundation, and then build from there.

Good luck!

Chapter 1

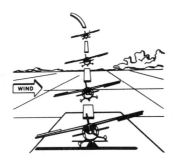

The Four Fundamentals

Just four fundamentals are the foundation on which all forms of flight are built. These four most basic flight techniques are *straight and level, climbs, turns,* and *glides.* If you want to become a precise pilot, you must master the basic flight maneuvers to the point that they become automatic and instinctive. You see, every single maneuver you will ever do in an aircraft has its origins in the four fundamentals. I can think of no aerial maneuver (not even in aerobatics) that does not rely directly on a precise knowledge of these basic flight techniques. They are so important to the process of learning to fly that I believe any pilot who does not master them will most certainly be less than a complete pilot. He may, in fact, be dangerous both to himself and to others who have the ill fortune to fly with him—or get run over by him.

You see, to most people who consider learning to fly, taking off and landing seem to be the only things to be mastered. How very wrong they are! These are the same people who sometimes want to hurry through the basics so they can get on with the interesting part—takeoffs and landings. It is also this type who, more often than not, end up as statistics—*bad* statistics, like dead. Don't get caught in this trap. Learn from the beginning; don't start in the middle.

If you don't master the four fundamentals, you will find yourself having trouble with all subsequent maneuvers. This is because, as I have said, all maneuvers have their origins in the four basics. I have had students tell me that they were having an inordinate amount of trouble with some advanced maneuver such as a chandelle. I ask them to explain exactly what sort of trouble they are experiencing with the maneuver, and the reply is usually something to the effect that they can't seem to get the maneuver to "come out right." They can do certain parts of the maneuver one-at-a-time, but can't seem to put it all together. They may, for instance, be able to start the turn portion of the maneuver, but when they add the climb portion to the already-established turn, they lose control of the bank involved and the maneuver goes down the tubes. The problem? They have not yet mastered climbing turns!

You should see the looks on the faces of 200-hour pilots when I tell them they should go back and work—*really* work—on climbing turns. They usually look at me like I was crazy. Have I not just insulted their piloting ability? Not really. Actually, I feel as if I have done them a great favor—one they won't really appreciate until they return to work on the basic maneuver that was causing all the others to be troublesome. Only after working out the kinks in the basics will the advanced maneuver fall into place as it should. Then, and only then, will it dawn on them as to the importance of mastering the basics of flight. Then they are really ready to become precise pilots.

This sort of problem is all too common in aviation. Some people are in too big a hurry to get on to the finished product without laying the proper groundwork. To me, that's like trying to put a roof on a house that has yet to be built. You just can't do it, but many people continue to try. They fail and then don't seem to understand why. Sometimes they don't even understand after being told the reasons for their failures. Maybe they just don't want to hear it, or maybe their egos are too big to admit that they should return to basic work even after they have accumulated many flight hours.

Now we know the problem, but where do we find the solution? I maintain the solution is placed almost exclusively in the hands of our flight instructors. It is up to them to maintain high standards of learning, watch for those prospective pilots who are in too big a hurry, and wise them up to the unequaled need to master basic flight before attempting further endeavors in flight training.

It also falls upon each individual (such as your reading this book) to seek out information and guidance that will help in mastering the fundamentals of flight one-step-at-a-time. In doing this, flight instructor and student can work together to obtain the desired end result—precision flight.

STRAIGHT AND LEVEL

Straight and level flight is usually the first maneuver you are introduced to as you learn to fly, and is the most elemental. It is, after all, the position in which you will spend the majority of your time as a pilot. For this reason alone it is important that you master the elements involved in straight and level flight.

The best definition of straight and level flight that I have ever come across is: slight corrections for any climb, turn, or dive. That means exactly what it says. You, the pilot, must constantly be aware of your attitude and make any appropriate adjustments to maintain that attitude. It means that if your heading wanders, you bring it back—now. It also means that if you start to climb or dive, you bring it back to level—now. These problems can easily be brought under control if you learn a bit about the visual and instrument clues you have at your disposal to aid your attitude references (Figs. 1-1, 1-2).

When you are in straight and level flight you will not be climbing, diving, or turning. This is the time to take a look at your attitude (which is to say, the attitude of your aircraft in relation to the ground). Look over the nose and note the relationship between the top of the engine cowl and the horizon. Try to take a mental picture of the scene in front of you, for this is how straight and level flight should look through the front window. If the scene changes—for instance, you notice more earth in your windshield than was there before—your pitch has changed and you are no longer flying level. In this case—more earth in the windshield—you are in a slight dive. On the other hand, if you notice less earth and more sky in your windshield, you are in a slight climb. In either case you will want to make an immediate pitch change to return to the desired straight and level attitude.

The wing tips will also help you to fly by an attitude. As you fly along straight and level, glance at one of the wing tips and notice its relation to the horizon. The wing tip and the horizon should be nearly parallel if you are in straight and level flight. Any subsequent change of pitch will be reflected by a change in the angle between the wing tip and the horizon. In other words, if the front of the wing tip appears to be closer to the horizon than the rear, you are diving; if the rearward edge of the wing tip appears closer to the horizon than the leading edge, then you are in a climb. Simple huh?

The wing tips can also tell you a great deal about laterally level flight. This is the roll axis, or the tilting from side to side—in layman's language, leaning. As you look out from the cockpit while

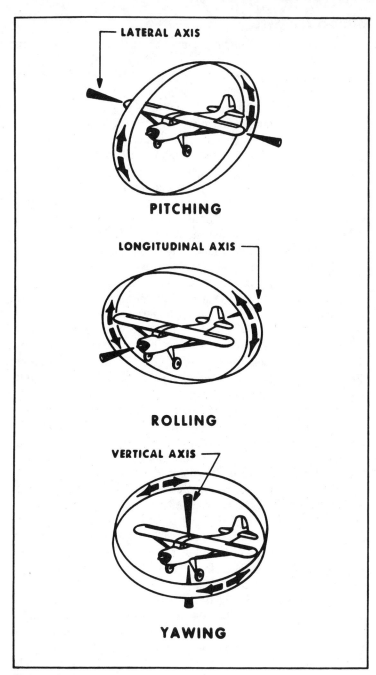

LATERAL AXIS

PITCHING

LONGITUDINAL AXIS

ROLLING

VERTICAL AXIS

YAWING

Fig. 1-1. Axes of an airplane. (courtesy FAA)

4

Fig. 1-2. Straight and level flight is defined as small corrections for roll, pitch, and yaw. (courtesy Cessna)

in straight and level flight, notice the distance between the bottom of the wing tip and the horizon. Take a mental picture of it and then look to the other wing tip. There you should see the same amount of distance between the wing tip and the horizon. If the distances are unequal, you are not in laterally level flight; you are in a wing-low attitude. If you stay in this wing-low attitude for any length of time you will begin to turn. Since you don't want to turn, you must correct the situation by turning the yoke in the direction of the *up* wing (the one with the most distance between the wing tip and the horizon). Just turn the yoke (wheel) slightly in the direction of the up wing as you add a small amount of rudder in the same direction. When the distance returns to the desired amount, return the aileron and rudder controls to the neutral position and you have corrected the roll problem—for now. I say "for now" because (much the same as in driving a car) an airplane usually won't stay where you put it for long. You must be continually monitoring your position and taking prompt corrective action when things begin to wander.

The two methods just discussed are the best I know to correct errors in pitch and roll using the visual method of attitude flying. Remember that the position of your aircraft in relation to the horizon is the key; learn to use your reference points and make them work for you until they are a firmly established portion of your attitude flying technique.

To properly learn attitude flying, you must learn to incorporate the visual references you see outside the aircraft with the references you get from the instruments on the panel. These instruments will tell you exactly what attitude you are in at any given time—the same as your visual references do, except they are mechanical. To really learn to fly with precision, you must use both outside visual references (VR) and your instrument references (IR). This means that you should not use one set of references so much that the other is left unused; doing so can lead to some big problems in safety. For example, if you fly around staring at the gauges, you won't see what is going on around you and you just might run into something or somebody. This is not good for your health or longevity.

The best way to avoid problems is to use both IR and VR references to complement each other—to use one to check against the other so you get used to both methods and develop a safer, more precise flight technique.

Let's say you are flying along straight and level, looking at your wing tips and the view over the nose to check for your proper references. Everything is going fine; all reference points are where they are supposed to be. Now glance inside and sneak a peek at your attitude indicator. It should show wings level and the little airplane (this is you) should be right on the horizon—no bank, no pitch; straight and level. Next glance at your airspeed indicator. It should show a constant airspeed. Your vertical speed indicator should read zero and your altimeter should read a constant altitude. If all these instruments agree with what you saw through the windshield, then you are indeed in straight and level flight and have cross-checked your instruments with your visual references.

Suppose you are in what you *believe* to be straight and level flight, visually, but when you look at the instruments you find the vertical speed indicator shows a descent and your airspeed is above normal cruise for straight and level flight. What does this tell you? It *should* tell you that your visual references are not quite right and you are diving. Just bring your nose up a little and then check your instruments again. If all is well, take another look outside and try to reestablish your outside visual references. Do you begin to see how this works? You must use one set of references to check the other. In this way you can begin to really get a feel for attitude flying and start to recognize the importance of the instrument cross-check with the visual references.

CLIMBS

Climbs are another of the four basic fundamentals that you

must master on your road to becoming a precise pilot. Climbs, as with straight and level (and all maneuvers, for that matter), should be practiced until you can accomplish them smoothly using both VR and IR references in combination.

Many of the same reference points used in straight and level flight may be used for climbs. Wing tips can be used to complement instrument indications for laterally level flight, and also for pitch information. I teach my students to set up a climb attitude and then trim the aircraft for hands-off flight (Fig. 1-3). I then have them look to the wing tips and witness the angle of the wings to the horizon in order to get a visual picture of the climb attitude. (In most trainer aircraft you are usually sitting either directly under or on top of the wings, so you can get a very good visual pitch reference.)

Fig. 1-3. The normal climb attitude of a Cessna 152.

In most aircraft you will lose the entire forward view of the horizon in a climb attitude. For this reason, the flight instruments (particularly your directional gyro) are very important in maintaining your directional control. The wing tips, however, may still be used for directional reference if you learn to use them properly.

After getting established in a climb attitude, gently apply rudder pressure in first one direction and then the other. Keep watching the wing tips; they will appear to move forward and backward as your rudder pressure is applied to the left and then to the right. If you see them moving, you had a reference point picked out whether you knew it or not. Merely keep the wing parallel to the reference point and you will keep your heading pretty well on-target. If you keep your wing tip on a single point, however, such as a tree, you will wind up going around in a circle. As you can see, a small amount of common sense must accompany this method.

I have found a distant road, railroad track, or section line to be very useful in this wing tip heading management—but they had better be parallel to your course or you might wind up in Toledo.

As you continue to master VR and IR climbs, don't forget to use your trim tab to help maintain constant pitch and airspeed control. If

Fig. 1-4. For every action there is an equal, but opposite, reaction. (courtesy FAA)

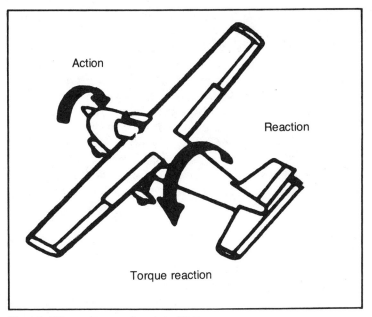

Fig. 1-5. Effects of torque. (courtesy FAA)

you find yourself yawing to the left (*yaw* is a turn without bank), you have probably forgotten to make a correction for torque and P-factor with your right rudder.

Torque is defined as "any rolling or twisting motion." It is present in all propeller-driven aircraft and is a prime example of the law that "For every action there is an equal but opposite reaction (Fig. 1-4)."

When your propeller turns, it causes *action*. Since the propeller is attached to the aircraft, the *reaction* comes in the form of the aircraft trying to roll, or twist, in the opposite direction (Fig. 1-5). Since most American-made aircraft of the single-engine variety have a propeller that turns clockwise as viewed from the cockpit, the action is also clockwise. But the reaction is *counterclockwise* and the resultant yaw is to the left.

Torque is present any time the propeller is turning. It varies in intensity only by changing rpm. You don't notice the effects of torque in straight and level flight because the aircraft is rigged so no correction is needed at normal cruise power settings and at cruising airspeed.

P-factor, on the other hand, is only present in attitudes other than straight and level. It comes into play during climbs and descents. It, as with torque, tends to yaw the aircraft to the left when in a climbing attitude.

P-factor yaws the aircraft due to unequal thrust. The aircraft is pulled through the air by the propeller, which is an airfoil; it acts very much like a wing except that it is rotating. As it rotates in straight and level flight, both propeller blades get an equal "bite" of air, which produces an equal amount of thrust from each blade. When you are in a climbing attitude, however, the descending blade (the one on the right when viewed from the cockpit) has a much larger angle of attack than the ascending blade. This larger angle of attack gives the descending blade more effective thrust than the ascending blade and so you have the two propeller blades creating unequal thrust (Fig. 1-6). This unequal thrust causes the aircraft to yaw to the left.

The proper corrective action to offset the effects of torque or P-factor is to apply right rudder in amounts only as needed to help you maintain your heading.

As you practice climbs, don't forget to keep a sharp eye out for other traffic; turn every so often so you don't fly too long partially blinded by your nose-high attitude. Also, don't forget to use your trim tab to help with precise airspeed control.

DESCENTS

Descents, or glides, are the third of the four fundamentals and

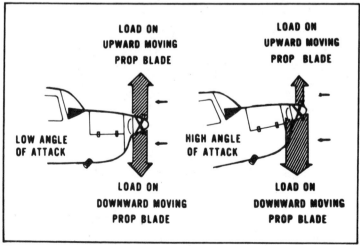

Fig. 1-6. P-factor results from an unequal thrust from the propeller blades during a climb. (courtesy FAA)

should be honed to perfection. Too many pilots are inclined to merely push the nose down and let the chips fall where they may. While this will get the job done, it is *not* the best way to obtain maximum performance from your aircraft. If you like thrills, go ride on some rides at a carnival or take aerobatics, because it is very unwise to dive your civilian trainer to near-redline speeds— *especially* in turbulent air. You could start out playing dive-bomber and wind up playing Kamikaze. This could really spoil your weekend plans.

In teaching descents, I have my students use the two most-used types of normal descent procedures. One is the cruise-type descent; the other is the approach-to-landing descent.

I guess it doesn't really matter which one you master first, as long as they are both practiced and understood. The cruise descent is used mainly in cross-country work and is used to reduce your altitude gradually over a rather long span of time and distance. Like all other aspects of precise flight, it requires practice and preplanning to become a good habit.

Let's assume you are arriving in the vicinity of your destination airport after a cross-country flight and you have to let down to a sea level airport from your cruising altitude of 5000 feet. Let's say you have found 500 feet per minute (fpm) to be a comfortable descent rate in your aircraft. From your 5000-ft. cruising altitude it will take you about 10 minutes to get down. How far out will you need to begin your descent in order to arrive at your destination airport at the traffic pattern altitude? If your destination airport has a 1000-ft. traffic pattern, you will have to lose 4000 ft. At 500 fpm it should take you about eight minutes.

Now you know that it will take eight minutes to descend from your cruising altitude to your pattern altitude. How far will you go in eight minutes? This is of course dependent on your ground speed. Remember, it's your ground speed, *not* your airspeed, that will give you the most accurate information. If you do not know your ground speed, indicated airspeed will give you a pretty close estimate unless you have a very strong wind.

For simplicity, let's say you have a ground speed of 120 mph and eight minutes to lose 4000 ft. Since 120 mph equates to two miles per minute and you have eight minutes to get down, you merely multiply the miles per minute by the minutes of descent in order to find out at what distance to initiate your descent. In this case it would be $2 \times 8 = 16$. You would begin your 500-fpm descent 16 miles out in order to arrive at your destination airport at a

1000-ft. traffic pattern altitude. That's much more precise than trial and error, isn't it?

In order to execute this descent in this precision manner, you will have to practice in your particular aircraft until you find the combination of power, trim, and airspeed that will give you the most satisfactory results. My students learn this procedure in the following manner.

Start at normal cruise speed, at a given altitude, and slowly reduce your power as you trim the aircraft to maintain the cruise speed. With the power reduced, and maintaining the same airspeed, you can't help but start to descend. Now watch the vertical speed indicator as you begin your descent. When it settles on your desired rate, adjust your trim and power to hold it there and then sit back and watch for other traffic as you practice your cruise descent.

The other type of descent is, I feel, even more important to student pilots. It is the normal approach descent. This descent will help you in several areas since it not only teaches you one method of getting down, but also helps you gain the feel for your aircraft in approach configuration at approach airspeed. It is also a little more precise maneuver than the cruise descent, because you not only have to adjust power and trim but also use the flaps and gear as well as continue to monitor other traffic. In short, it's more work. But in this instance, more work will help you develop your pilot technique to a higher standard.

The approach descent can be accomplished in a number of different configurations. For simplicity we will cover the technique I use to teach in a Cessna 152; with only minor modifications, this method may be used for most general aviation aircraft.

Starting at a given heading, altitude, and airspeed, slowly reduce the power to about 1500 rpm and hold enough back pressure on the stick to maintain a level flight attitude. As the airplane slows, begin trimming to relieve the pressure on the stick as you put down whatever flap setting you choose to practice on this particular configuration. (My students use everything from clean to full-flap configurations in order to practice in a diversified variety of conditions.)

As the airspeed slows to approach speed, keep the power constant and trim for hands-off flight. The nose will start to lower and you will be in an approach descent. The rate of descent is usually controlled with the power; the airspeed is controlled with the pitch. In other words, if you see you are descending too fast, you can either bring the pitch up a little, add a touch of power, or both.

You will have to work a little to find the right combinations, especially in rough air. It is worthwhile work, however, because of the great gain you will be achieving in the feel of your aircraft as well as utilizing both IR and VR references.

Practice both types of descents straight ahead and in turns in both directions. This will sharpen your skills in airspeed and attitude control and help your turns while descending in the traffic pattern (Fig. 1-7).

TURNS

Speaking of turns, it has been my observation that turns are very high on the list of aviation maneuvers *least* understood by many pilots. Needless to say, this lack of knowledge entails problems in many areas of flight that depend on proper turn technique to complete a given task. Turns also happen to be the fourth of the four basic flight fundamentals that must be mastered before you can even dream of becoming a precise pilot.

Almost everything in the world—*including* the world—turns. But few things turn like an aircraft. Turning your aircraft is different from turning your car, your boat, your chair, or your head. Turning an aircraft is unique. When you are flying, *fly*. Don't drive, steer, point or aim—fly!

Unless you happen to be an aeronautical engineer, you probably don't care *why* an airplane turns, but you had better care *how* it turns because you are the one who is going to have to get the job done.

Fig. 1-7. A landing is merely the culmination of a descent.

Coordination is the key that unlocks the door to a well-executed turn. It takes coordination of the hands, feet, eyes, and mind to properly turn an aircraft—a *learned* coordination developed by many hours of practice. I have never seen a student get into an aircraft and turn it properly the first time. It takes time and practice to really learn to turn an aircraft properly.

Although somewhat different from the way you turn your car, turning an aircraft is not really difficult. The main thing to remember is that you are in an aircraft, not in your car. Almost every student has, at one time or another, attempted to twist the yoke off the panel while trying to turn the aircraft as if it were a car. This happens most often during the early stages of dual and usually on the ground during taxi practice. The student will come upon a corner and either turn or use the prop as a weed mower. If you think I'm kidding, just wander around your local airport sometime this summer. The aircraft used as primary trainers will be the ones with the ragweed and Johnson grass dangling from the wheel pants and the greenish tinge on the edges of the prop.

On the ground the aircraft is taxied at a slow walk and turned with the use of the rudder pedals. The rudder pedals are connected to the nosewheel and provide steering through all ground movements. The brakes should be used only as necessary and are never held on during taxi, as this can cause the brake discs to overheat and warp. Remember: Rudders are for directional control; brakes are for stopping.

In the air, however, the aircraft is turned with the coordinated use of the ailerons, rudder, and elevator. The word *coordinated* is of the utmost importance, because if you so desired, you could turn the aircraft with only the ailerons or the rudder. This is not desirable, however, since it does not produce maximum performance from your aircraft.

An aircraft turns because of lift. It is actually lifted through a turn by the increase and decrease of lift from the opposing wings. Maybe it is easier to understand if you think of it in terms of *a change in the direction of lift* from straight up to an angle relative to the horizon. This change is implemented with the ailerons and produces the bank that then lifts the aircraft in another direction and results in a turn.

A properly coordinated level turn is accomplished when the aileron and rudder are used simultaneously, causing the aircraft to bank to the desired degree (Figs. 1-8, 1-9). A small amount of back pressure is added to the elevator to keep the nose up and maintain

Fig. 1-8. A Cessna 152 in a level left turn. (courtesy Cessna)

altitude. When the desired amount of bank is reached, everything (except the elevator) is returned to neutral to stop the aircraft in the desired bank. If you were to hold the aileron and rudder in the aircraft would continue to bank further, and neither you nor your trainer aircraft are probably ready for rolls.

The elevator must be kept slightly aft of neutral to maintain altitude during the turn, because any time the aircraft is in a banked

Fig. 1-9. Surprise! A Cessna Citation II turns just like the Cessna 152, only it goes faster. (courtesy Cessna)

situation, it loses some vertical lift. The result of losing vertical lift, if not corrected, is the nose of the aircraft dropping and the loss of altitude during the turn. During a prolonged turn, you make up for aft elevator by adjusting the elevator trim tab slightly to maintain your attitude and altitude.

I said above that an aircraft should be turned through the coordinated use of the controls even though it *could* be turned with only the ailerons *or* the rudder. Why, then, would we want to make it harder and add both controls when either would do the job? It's simple: You want coordination and maximum performance from your aircraft. This is the main thing every pilot is trying to achieve; to make his aircraft go *where* he wants it to go, *when* he wants it to, is the goal of every precise pilot.

If the ailerons produce the rolling motion, then what is the rudder for? It is put on your aircraft for two very good reasons: One is to allow control over the *yaw,* or side-to-side movement of the aircraft. The other is to overcome adverse yaw produced by the ailerons during the turn entry.

Try this little experiment the next time you fly and I think you will gain some insight into turns: Fly straight and level and place your feet on the floor. Pick a prominent object or reference point over the nose and roll into a turn without the use of rudder. The nose will seem to actually go in the *opposite* direction for an instant, and then it will resume its normal flight path. This phenomenon is called *adverse yaw,* and is caused by the drag of the down aileron before it generates enough lift to overcome that drag. It may be clearly seen and should be remembered as how *not* to turn an aircraft, as well as a wonderful method of visual reference.

Now reverse the process and roll into a turn using the same reference point. This time purposely lead the turn with the rudder and then apply your aileron. The result will be the nose yawing in the direction of the turn, followed by the roll induced by the aileron. You should see a clear picture of an uncoordinated turn. Hopefully, the result of all this uncoordination will be to instill the habit of monitoring your coordination through the use of both IR and VR references (Fig. 1-10).

In a properly coordinated level turn, using outside visual references, the nose of your aircraft will roll about a point and then continue in the direction of the turn.

Now combine all the basic maneuvers—straight and level, climbs, glides, and turns—and practice them by doing climbing and descending turns left and right in different configurations,

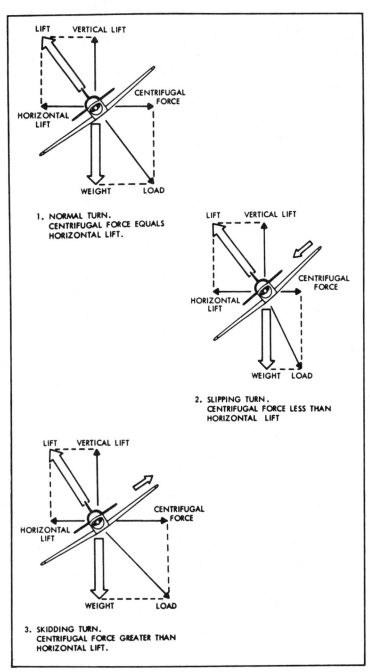

Fig. 1-10. Forces at work in normal, slipping, and skidding turns. (courtesy FAA)

17

airspeeds, and flap settings. Get the feel of your aircraft and of your coordination. Remember, only when you have mastered the basics can you continue on and work toward becoming a really precise pilot. Never forget for a moment that every single maneuver you will ever do will be made up of one, or a combination, of the four fundamentals. They *must* be mastered.

Chapter 2

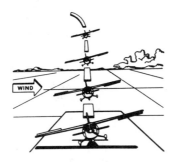

Basic Maneuvers

Slow flight is one of the two maneuvers that separates the pilots from the aircraft drivers; it will invariably show whether or not a pilot has a true feel for his aircraft. Slow flight, when properly performed, is a supreme blend of man and machine performing at the very limits of sustained flight. True slow flight, performed at minimum controllable airspeed, shows the difference between flying the aircraft with precision and skill, and wallowing around the sky hunting for your original heading, altitude, and airspeed. It is the fine line that separates controlled flight from a stall.

SLOW FLIGHT

In slow flight (which I define as anything less than cruise), as the airspeed decreases, so does control effectiveness. As the aircraft slows, more control travel is required to obtain the same results as at normal cruise speed. The reason for this is the lessening of the airflow over the airfoil as the airspeed is decreased.

One factor that many pilots forget is that the reverse of this is also true as the aircraft is gaining speed during the takeoff roll. When the takeoff roll is initiated, the pilot has little control of the airfoils since there is little or no air flowing over them. As the speed is increased, however, the control surfaces become more effective as more air flows over their surfaces. It is a fact of flight that the more air you have flowing over your control surfaces, the greater your control will be—and as the airflow becomes less and less, the more control effectiveness you will lose.

Slow flight, if taken seriously, is much more than just an exercise to practice for a check ride. It is a safety measure that is used nearly all the time your aircraft is operating at less-than-normal cruise speed. This would include the takeoff roll, climbout, descent, and approach to landing—right down to touchdown. It is a maneuver that should be taken very seriously (Fig. 2-1).

Learning to master slow flight is no more difficult than learning to master any other particular maneuver. You will want to start out at a safe altitude on a given heading and airspeed and then maintain the altitude and heading as you slow the aircraft to begin your slow flight practice. (*Note:* I tell my students that a safe altitude to practice slow flight is at least 2500 ft. AGL.)

As you reduce power to slow the aircraft, add back pressure on the elevator to maintain altitude and level flight attitude. If you don't do this the aircraft will just nose over and head for the dirt. As this transition is taking place, be sure to use the elevator trim to alleviate any control pressure on the yoke. A byproduct of good trim use is the tremendous help you receive in keeping your airspeed constant.

When the aircraft will no longer hold its altitude in level flight attitude, you will have to increase your pitch to help make up for the lessening angle of attack. Use power, pitch, and trim as needed to maintain your airspeed and altitude; use whatever power and pitch changes you need to get the job done. One of the foremost problems

Fig. 2-1. A Cessna 152 in no-flap slow flight. (courtesy Cessna)

that inhibits good slow flight technique is a shyness many pilots have in the use of these controls. They tend to get behind their aircraft and then it's a roller-coaster ride trying to catch up. Stay on top of the situation.

Generally speaking, power controls your altitude and pitch controls your airspeed during slow flight. Naturally, when you change one, you will have to change the other—but only slightly. If you are really keeping up, a small change in power will probably be all you need to counteract a slight climb or descent, just as a slight change of pitch will usually cure a small change in your airspeed. Remember the trim and let it work for you. Strive for hands-off flight in all attitudes and your airspeed control will probably take care of itself.

One other very important aspect to consider is the effect of torque and P-factor during slow flight. Any time you are in a nose-up, power-on attitude, you will have to correct for these two rascals. If you wonder why your slow flight headings are often somewhere to the right of where you actually are, remember the correction for torque and P-factor. All you need is a little right rudder and your problem will evaporate. Use just enough rudder to maintain your heading; don't turn your aircraft with your rudder. In this maneuver, think of your rudder input as a lateral trim tab.

Full-Flap Slow Flight

Now that you've got the basic slow flight procedure down pat, it's time to complicate matters a little. Try some slow flight using different flap settings. I have my students practice slow flight in every conceivable configuration—full flap, partial flap, no flap, and everything I can find in between. With this procedure they obtain a good feel for the aircraft in as many different configurations as we can find. If you have an aircraft with retractable gear, so much the better. Intersperse gear-up and gear-down configurations with the flaps to add even more challenge to the task.

As you know, when flaps are added, the nose of the aircraft has a tendency to rise. It will do the same in slow flight, so be ready for it. React to the pitch change even as it happens and add enough forward pressure on the yoke to maintain your attitude as you trim off the pressure with the elevator trim tab.

I have a very strong opinion about full-flap slow flight. I say you are cheating and kidding yourself if you think full-flap slow flight is done correctly by slowing your aircraft into the white arc (flap operating range on your airspeed indicator) and then applying full flaps while the aircraft shudders and creaks from the sudden drag of the flaps and slows down to the desired airspeed. You are cheating yourself out of all the other intermediate configurations. Is not your flap extension handle marked with different settings? Of course it is, and the different settings are used for different purposes. Why not be ready for any eventuality?

I further maintain that I could take someone who had never seen an aircraft before and have him performing slow flight of the sudden zero-to-full-flap variety in about 15 minutes. Of course, he would be performing by rote; very little learning would have occured. Would you want to share your airspace with him?

I believe that only by practicing slow flight in *every* conceivable configuration are you really able to get a feel for your aircraft and learn its good points and peculiarities. It will allow you to be more comfortable during an approach to landing, while climbing out after takeoff, or any other time in which you might be maneuvering at less than normal cruise airspeed (Fig. 2-2). It will make you more precise.

Slow Flight Turns

It is also an excellent idea for you to practice slow flight turns, climbs, and glides. This adds to your knowledge of your capabilities and those of your aircraft. One of the primary objectives of slow flight maneuvering practice is the maintenance of a given airspeed while turning, climbing, or descending. To maintain a given airspeed during slow flight you must continually monitor your attitude, adjust power, pitch, and trim, and correct for the effects of torque, all the while staying on the lookout for other traffic. Gets busy, doesn't it?

Fig. 2-2. An approach and landing is actually a form of slow flight.

STALL SPEEDS — MPH CAS				
Gross Weight 1600 lbs. CONDITION	ANGLE OF BANK			
	0°	20°	40°	60°
Flaps UP	55	57	63	78
Flaps 20°	49	51	56	70
Flaps 40°	48	49	54	67
POWER OFF — AFT CG				

Fig. 2-3. Stall speed chart clearly shows how the aircraft angle of bank and configuration affect stalling speed. (courtesy FAA)

In a slow flight turn you treat the aircraft *almost* as you would in a normal cruise turn. The biggest difference is that you will want to use a shallow bank. The reasons for this are fairly obvious: First, you are flying at a speed only slightly above stall speed. Second, as your bank increases, your stall speed increases proportionately (Fig. 2-3). When you add these two factors together you will see that since you are flying slowly to begin with, any significant bank increase can bring you into a situation where a stall is very likely. Hence, use a shallow bank in slow flight.

You will also find that your aircraft will turn to the left much easier than it will to the right. This is because torque and P-factor are already trying to pull the aircraft to the left in your nose-high, power-on situation. You correct for this left turn tendency with right rudder to maintain your heading, so in order to turn to the left, about all you need do is ease off some of the right rudder; the aircraft should slowly start to turn to the left. A turn to the right is as per normal except that you need a bit more right rudder than you would in a normal cruise turn—again, to overcome the effects of torque and P-factor.

Too many pilots get into trouble because they can't seem to fly an aircraft slowly and still maintain a safe margin of control. The art of maneuvering your aircraft with diminished control response is of utmost importance. Your reactions must be correct, instinctive, and honed to perfection. I recommend intensive practice on slow flight at regular intervals if you want to be really safe and precise.

STALLS

Closely coupled with your slow flight techniques will be your stall recognition and recovery techniques. Stall/spin accidents are high on the list of causal factors for aircraft accidents—for both IFR and VFR flight. And many, if not *most,* of these accidents are preventable. They can be prevented by pilots being educated in stall recognition and recovery techniques. But don't just learn about stalls for a given checkride and then forget them. They must be a part of every good pilot's learning process, but should also be practiced at regular intervals throughout a flying career.

Simply stated, an aircraft cannot stall unless it exceeds the critical angle of attack. Remember, the angle of attack is the angle between the chord line of the wing and the relative wind. Most airfoils become critical somewhere between 15 and 20 degrees of pitch. Don't exceed your critical angle of attack and you will never stall—never.

It's that simple, and yet people continue to stall, spin, and crash. Maybe it's because they have become complacent, or maybe they are in a hurry and forget the skills they learned some time back. Maybe they have not had to push themselves and their aircraft to the limit for a long time. The possibilities are many and varied, but I believe the problem stems from a lack of familiarity with stall recognition and recovery technique. If you recognize an approaching stall and take prompt corrective action, you won't have any worry about stall recovery since you will have alleviated the problem long before any stall occurs. If you *do* allow a stall to proceed through the full break, you will have to take quick, correct action, so learn and practice all recognition and recovery techniques for stalls from any anticipated situation.

The Accelerated Stall

The accelerated stall occurs when the critical angle of attack is exceeded by abrupt control movement, causing the aircraft to stall at a higher-than-normal airspeed. Just because your aircraft has a V_{so} (power off stall speed with your gear and flaps down) of 40 doesn't mean that there is no way of stalling it at a higher airspeed if you exceed the critical angle of attack. And you don't necessarily have to be in a nose-high attitude to stall your aircraft, either.

You can stall an aircraft going straight up, straight down, or straight and level, for that matter, if you exceed the critical angle of attack. This is something that bears repeating. Many pilots are of the mistaken notion that their aircraft will not stall unless they are in a nose-high attitude. Wrong! The unfortunate part of this erroneous thinking is that it creates premature funerals. Remember, an airfoil will stall *any* time its critical angle of attack is exceeded, at any airspeed. In an accelerated stall, it's going to happen to you at a higher-than-normal airspeed; it will usually require some very rapid control movement to induce the stall, but it *will* stall (Fig. 2-4).

Everything has its limits and so does your aircraft. For example, what is the highest airspeed at which you may stall your aircraft safely? It's *maneuvering speed*—the speed at which you may apply full, abrupt control travel without causing structural damage to your aircraft. Any time you are at or below maneuvering speed you can stall your aircraft without any worry about structural failure. It is a built-in safety factor tested by the manufacturer and certified in your aircraft's operation limitations section of the operating handbook. But please don't rush out and try it. Take my word for it for now and get a little more acquainted with stalls and their characteristics before deciding if you really want to try it. I personally have never tried it except in our aerobatic aircraft.

To practice accelerated stalls, first climb to minimum stall

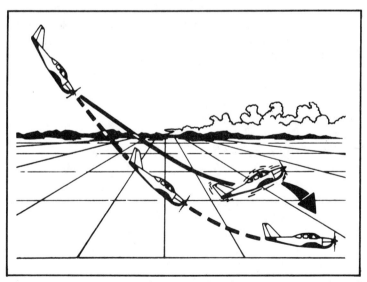

Fig. 2-4. Increasing the angle of attack too abruptly can cause an accelerated stall. (courtesy FAA)

recovery altitude of 1500 feet AGL—and then climb another couple thousand feet to allow for mistakes. Clear the area by making a couple of 90-degree turns or a single 180, whichever makes you happy. Be sure to *look* for other aircraft while you are doing your clearing turns. Too many pilots go through the motions of clearing turns and then spend the time they should be using to look for other aircraft to adjust the cabin ventilation or blow their nose or something. The purpose of clearing turns is to make *very* sure you don't have any company.

The entry speed for an accelerated stall should be no more than 1¼ times the unaccelerated stall speed in a clean configuration: V_{S1} times 1.25. In other words, if your aircraft had a V_{S1} of 60 knots, this would work out to an entry speed of 75 knots. This rather low speed provides for a margin of safety since the load factor at the time of the stall will be lower if the stall is initiated at $1.25 \times V_{S1}$ than up near maneuvering speed. The resultant stall will be less violent and will cause less stress on both you and the aircraft.

After arriving at your altitude and clearing the area, slow your aircraft down to entry speed while maintaining your altitude and heading. Using a rather low power setting, roll into a 45-degree bank and rapidly pull back on the yoke. The aircraft should begin to turn, shudder, and then stall at an airspeed much higher than normal. If properly executed, it should stall rather quickly and break rather sharply. If you turn more than 90 degrees during the execution of an accelerated stall, you aren't pulling back rapidly enough on the yoke and aren't getting a true accelerated stall. You don't have time to eat a hamburger while doing an accelerated stall. It happens in a hurry—that's how it got its name.

Recovery from an accelerated stall is as with all stalls:

1. Reduce the pitch to break the stall.
2. Add power, if available.
3. Level the wings and return to normal flight attitude.

Complete these procedures in the above order—and quickly. The stall recovery may be initiated at any of the normal recognition cues peculiar to stalls or impending stalls. These cues are common to all stalls and include the warning horn, light, decreasing control effectiveness, buffet, and the break. The most sinister thing about the accelerated stall is that these cues happen much more rapidly than is the case with most stalls. If you practice recovery at all the different cues, however, you will be ready should you ever get into a situation that calls for your prompt action.

Leveling the Wings

While on the subject of stalls and stall recovery techniques, I would like to point out something that I have observed over many years of flight instruction as one of the most common problem areas in stall recovery. It's the leveling of the wings. It's number three on the recovery checklist—last. And it's last for a very good reason. When an aircraft stalls, it's the airfoils that actually stall. The wings and the horizontal stabilizer stall and remain stalled until you release some of the back pressure and once again allow the air to return to a normal pattern flowing over the wings. I don't care how hard you try, you will not be able to level your wings with your ailerons until the stall is broken. The wings are stalled and your ailerons are attached to your wings, aren't they? They are useless until you break the stall—period.

It's a natural tendency to try to pick up a wing that has suddenly dropped off with the ailerons. I have seen students literally twist the yoke until it nearly broke off trying to regain level flight attitude while their wings were still stalled. It won't work, for the aforementioned reasons. What will? Your *rudder,* that's what. The rudder remains effective long after the other control surfaces have become useless, and it should be used to pick up a down wing during stall recovery. Of course you need to know which one to use, as applying incorrect rudder will simply aggravate the situation and possibly cause even more problems. Use the rudder *opposite* the down wing to initiate wings-level attitude during your initial stall recovery.

I'm *not* recommending the use of the rudder to the exclusion of your other flight controls during stall recovery. I simply mean that the rudder is the control that should be used first—to level your wings, that is. Then normal recovery is accomplished through the coordinated use of all available controls and power.

The Takeoff and Departure Stall

The *takeoff and departure stall* usually occurs due to a lack of pilot attention to pitch during this critical portion of flight. It is often caused by an overzealous pilot pitching his aircraft up to the point where this particular type of stall is almost unavoidable. Many of them, I suspect, may be trying to show off, or maybe they just aren't paying enough attention to their pitch and airspeed. At any rate, far too many accident reports carry this final notation: "Failed to obtain/maintain flying speed."

In order to practice recognition and recovery from this stall, climb to at least 1500 AGL and then add a couple thousand feet for error. Clear the area, as always, before practicing stalls.

The takeoff and departure stall is initiated at liftoff speed, so retard your throttle well below cruise rpm and maintain a constant altitude as your aircraft slows to liftoff speed. As you reach liftoff speed, advance your throttle to full takeoff power and simultaneously increase your pitch, not allowing any acceleration of your aircraft. After reaching the desired pitch, return all controls to neutral except for the rudder (right), which must be used to overcome torque and P-factor. Recovery may be initiated at the first sign of an impending stall or after a full break (Fig. 2-5).

The takeoff and departure stall should be practiced from a straight climb as well as turns in both directions. When you practice them in climbing turns, use a moderate bank of 15 to 20 degrees. Notice how the cues in this stall seem to come one at a time. You should be able to recover at any one of these cues. In fact, to a really competent pilot, these cues almost scream for action on his part. They are saying, "You had better do something, dummy, because if you don't I'm gonna get you into some serious trouble." Notice these cues. Feel for them. Practice their recognition.

The recovery from a takeoff and departure stall is as for all other stalls except for the power. Since you already have a high power setting, merely reduce your pitch to break the stall and level your wings with coordinated use of all of your controls. Then fly your aircraft out of the stall with as little loss of altitude as possible and set up a normal climbout. Don't hurry your recovery and induce

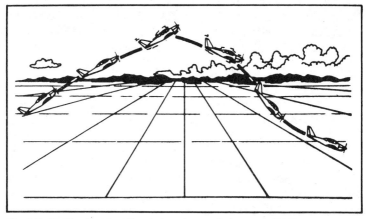

Fig. 2-5. Profile of a takeoff and departure stall. (courtesy FAA)

a secondary stall. Take it one step at a time and don't overwhelm yourself.

The Approach-to-Landing Stall

The approach-to-landing-stall often occurs on the turn from base leg to final approach, but it has been known to happen when a pilot attempts to stretch his glide on final without sufficient power to maintain altitude. The reason that the turn from base leg to final approach is the prime area for this stall is because some pilots often start their turn to final too late and are tempted to add a little inside rudder and some additional back pressure to try to tighten the turn. Seeing that this seems to help a little, but that they are still going to overshoot the runway centerline, they sneak in a little more rudder and back pressure in an attempt to tighten the turn even more. And to make matters worse, they almost always use some opposite aileron in an attempt to keep the turn from overbanking due to the effect of the rudder and back pressure. They are so intent on making the runway on the first try rather than going around and executing a better pattern that they fail to notice the cues the aircraft is giving them. They are in a flat, slipping turn at low altitude and airspeed—a perfect setup for an approach-to-landing-stall.

To safely practice approach-to-landing stalls, climb to an altitude considerably higher than the minimum recovery altitude of 1500 feet above the ground because you will be in a descent during this maneuver. Approach-to-landing stalls are executed from normal approach speed and should be practiced from straight glides as well as gliding turns. The turns help to simulate the turn from base leg to final approach. Practice both clean and full-flap configurations, since you may be called upon to make approaches in various configurations during the conduct of actual flight.

After carefully clearing the area, smoothly retard your throttle to approach power. Maintain your altitude as you slow to approach speed. During this time your flaps should be lowered to landing position (assuming your aircraft is so equipped). When normal approach speed is reached, initiate a descent and maintain this descent long enough for you to feel as though you are really on an approach. Then slowly increase your pitch as your power is reduced to idle. Continue to increase your pitch until the stall occurs. Usually, the stall will occur with very little nose-high attitude. Pulling the nose up too sharply ruins the intent of the maneuver, because after all, you don't pull your nose up quickly on a real approach, and the main thing you are after is realism, isn't it? Since this stall will almost invariably happen slowly and gradually, you should be able to feel and recognize the cues as they come one at a time.

Recovery from an approach-to-landing stall may be initiated at any point up to and including a full break. Recovery is much like a full-flap go-around from a landing approach. Back pressure is relaxed and power smoothly added as the wings are leveled and you go to your best angle-of-climb or best rate-of-climb airspeed. While you are transitioning from the approach to your climb attitude, bring the flaps up to the manufacturer's recommended setting for a go-around. In most aircraft, the flaps are *not* brought up all at once because this can cause a momentary sink that could prove to be very unhealthy at a low altitude.

As stated before, this stall should be practiced from gliding turns in both directions as well as straight ahead. When practicing them in turns, use a moderate bank of about 15 to 20 degrees and do not allow the bank to increase once you have initiated the maneuver. All other recovery procedures remain the same as for all stalls.

STEEP TURNS

Although not presently required for a Private Pilot Certificate, let's consider steep turns since so many flight instructors at least introduce them in primary flight.

Steep turns are another maneuver that demonstrates whether or not a pilot is truly master of his aircraft. Steep turns require an advanced sense of timing, coordination, and feel for your aircraft. Maintaining your altitude as well as your orientation are but two of the problems that the maneuver presents. Steep turns will take you and your aircraft to the opposite end of the spectrum from slow flight (Fig. 2-6). However, the possibility of a stall—an accelerated stall—still exists as your aircraft reaches the 50 to 60-degree bank range and large doses of back pressure are induced to help maintain your altitude.

The aviation industry seems to be divided on the subject of what really controls altitude during the conduct of steep turns. Many reputable pilots contend that back pressure alone controls the altitude, and I tend to agree with them—to a point. If, as you roll into a steep turn, you feed in *exactly* the right amount of back pressure, then I agree that it does control your altitude. However, pilots who can do this consistently are few and far between. Most pilots, during the entry to a steep turn, add either too much or too little back pressure and wind up chasing their altitude all the way

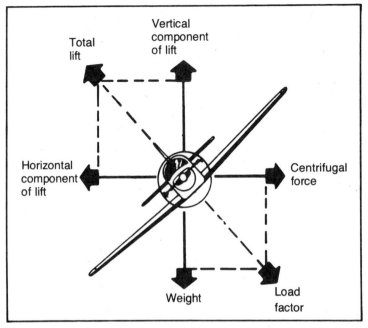

Fig. 2-6. Forces acting on an aircraft during a steep turn. (courtesy FAA)

around the turn. This results in what I call "720-degree vertical S-turns" that do very little for training and even less for the human stomach. The method I use incorporates both pitch and bank control to maintain altitude.

After clearing the area, set up straight and level flight below maneuvering speed. (Steep turns should be entered at or below maneuvering speed because of the possibility of inducing an accelerated stall with abrupt pitch changes at high bank angles.) Pick a heading and altitude at which to begin your steep turns. After completing a 360-degree or 720-degree steep turn, this will be the heading and altitude at which you want to wind up. You then begin the roll into the steep turn at a higher-than-normal rate. As the bank reaches about half of the desired amount—25 or 30 degrees—smoothly apply back pressure as you continue to roll to the desired amount of bank, about 50 to 60 degrees. If your back pressure input versus bank angle is relatively close to the desired amount, altitude may then be controlled by slight changes of bank to either increase or decrease the vertical lift. At the same time, small pitch changes may be necessary to complement the bank and aid in proper coordination.

Unless you're a master at steep turns or enjoy high G-loads and centrifugal force to the point that you may be in danger of pulling the fillings from your upper teeth, the vertical lift component can be taken care of with small changes in bank instead of large changes in pitch. Try it.

Since a steep turn will usually produce about two Gs, your airspeed will decay due to the higher load factor. Add power as needed to help keep the airspeed up. Remember, as the bank increases, so does your stall speed. Therefore, power application during your steep turn should help decrease your chances of an accelerated stall.

I have found that the most common problem associated with the steep turn is uncoordinated entry and recovery technique. A pilot entering with too little back pressure for a given bank will lose his effective lift due to the steep bank. The result is usually a

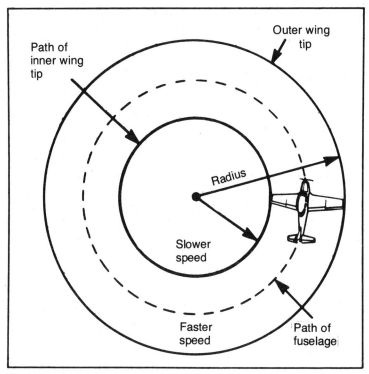

Fig. 2-7. In a turn, the outer wing must travel at a faster speed in order to cover the longer distance needed to stay up with the inner wing. The increased speed of the outer wing creates more lift and causes the aircraft to attempt to overbank during a steep turn. (courtesy FAA)

descending spiral. A pilot who enters with too much back pressure for a given bank will usually find himself in a tight, climbing turn. Proper application of rudder and aileron and the correct amount of back pressure will help assure a good entry into a steep turn.

Recovery from a steep turn is as with all turn recoveries, except that more control pressure will be required to make it come out in a coordinated fashion. Since you are turning at a high rate, it will take more rudder application than normal to overcome the turn and the adverse yaw of the ailerons as they are applied to reverse the bank. Also, as you are in the rollout, relax your back pressure to prevent a climb after the turn is completed. Too many pilots roll into a steep turn with a fine touch, fly the aircraft through two or three turns with seeming ease, and then forget to remove their back pressure proportionally as they are rolling out—they climb several hundred feet, which really looks great on a flight check. It shows that the pilot has not really mastered the precision needed to fully complete this maneuver—at least not mentally.

In order to keep a steep turn coordinated, a slight amount of opposite aileron must be used to overcome the overbanking tendency as your bank reaches the 50 to 60-degree range. Remember, a steep bank is one where the inherent stability of the aircraft causes it to keep on banking in a steep turn (Fig. 2-7). A little opposite aileron will stop this problem while keeping you coordinated. *Do not* use top rudder to correct the overbanking tendency. This will cause you to be in an uncoordinated, slipping turn. (The top rudder would be right rudder in a left turn or the left rudder in a right turn. Some pilots think of top rudder as the one closest to the sky during a turn.)

Chapter 3

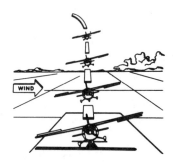

Ground Track Maneuvers

In all phases of aviation, you are at the mercy of the wind from the time you untie your aircraft until you safely tie it back down again. For this reason it is important that you become precise in all phases of aviation involving ground tracking procedures. Ground tracking is involved in your taxiing (Fig. 3-1), your takeoff and departure, your approach and landing, your navigation from point A to point B, and on and on. To me, ground tracking is the very essence of flight. It is important that you be able to go where you want to go, when you want to go, and to know that the wind will be nothing more than a small inconvenience and not something to be afraid of. In fact, the wind will often be of great service to you, such as a tailwind on a long cross-country. The point I'm trying to make is that you should learn to respect the wind, not fear it. A little of your time spent in really learning ground track techniques will reap tremendous dividends in the future as you grow into a really precise pilot.

TURNS-ABOUT-A-POINT

The *turn-about-a-point* is probably the most familiar ground reference maneuver to most pilots. Almost everyone has had to (or will have to) demonstrate this maneuver on one check ride or another. The problem is that all too many pilots work hard to get ready for a check ride—and then as soon as the ride is over, forget everything they ever knew about a maneuver or group of maneuvers. This is often the case with turns-about-a-point. The sad part is

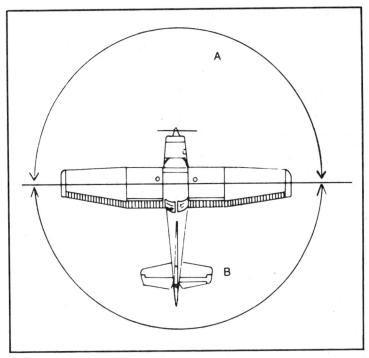

Fig. 3-1. Here's a simplified method of control positioning during taxi. If the wind is coming from in front of a line running from wing tip to wing tip, as in A, turn your yoke towards the wind. If the wind is blowing from behind the line, as in B, turn your yoke away from the wind. Simple, huh?

that the pilot who does this is really cheating himself and his passengers. He is cheating everyone out of a far safer and more precise flight, a flight that would be entirely uneventful because that pilot would be, indeed, the master of his aircraft.

Turns-about-a-point, as well as all other ground reference maneuvers, are entered downwind. The primary reason for the downwind entry is safety. Since your angle of bank is proportional to your ground speed, the faster your ground speed is, the steeper your bank will be. Conversely, the slower your ground speed, the shallower will be your bank. Therefore, if your turn-about-a-point is entered downwind, the initial bank will be the steepest that you will encounter in the maneuver. This keeps you from making the mistake of entering the maneuver upwind (into the wind) at a steep bank only to find that to hold the desired radius the bank may have to be increased to a point that may exceed the limitations of you or your aircraft.

All ground track maneuvers incorporate an infinite number of bank angles, but the three most used reference banks are *shallow, medium*, and *steep*. Once you have mastered the basic rules of bank as they apply to ground tracking, you should have no difficulty with any ground track maneuver.

The basic rules of bank are:

☐ Shallow bank upwind (wind in front of you).
☐ Medium bank crosswind (wind at your side).
☐ Steep bank downwind (wind behind you).

All of your other related banks will be made as you maneuver between these three main reference banks. Also, remember that the wing tips will be pointed at your reference point only when you are either directly upwind or downwind. Everywhere else your wing tips will be either ahead of or behind the reference point. *Do not* try to keep your wing tips on the reference point all the way around the circle or you will wind up with a very egg-shaped circle (Fig. 3-2). Crabbing is very important at all times other than when you are either directly upwind or downwind.

The turn-about-a-point may be either a very large circle, a very small circle, or somewhere in between. It all depends on how close you are to your reference point. The closer you are to your refer-

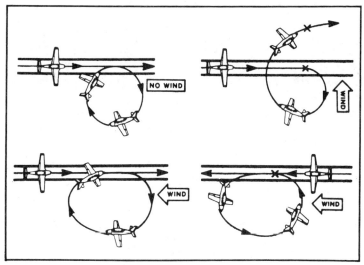

Fig. 3-2. The effects of the wind direction on your ground track during constant banked turns. (courtesy FAA)

ence point, the steeper your banks will be, and the smaller your circle will be. The farther away you are from your reference point, the shallower your banks will be, and your circle will be larger. You see, banks are relative to each other. Certainly a 45-degree bank is steeper than one of 15 degrees. But it is only three times as steep, whereas a bank of 5 degrees is five times as steep as a bank of 1 degree. So think of your banks as one relates to the other, not in terms of 10, 15, 45 degrees, etc. Think of them as shallow, medium, and steep.

To properly execute a turn-about-a-point, attain the proper altitude and clear the area of other traffic. Generally, you should be about 600 feet above any obstacles and over open country, then choose a point about which you wish to pivot. I mention open country because I once had a student, a real genius, who proceeded to take me over our city and began to execute turns-about-a-point over the local Catholic church steeple. Now, he did have a stationary point, and it was indeed easy to see, but at 600 feet over town, it was not only stupid, it was very illegal according to the FARs.

Anyway, after picking a readily visible stationary point, enter the turn-about-a-point downwind. Just as you cross abeam of the reference point, begin the bank. Your turn entry should be very coordinated and result in a steep bank. The steep bank will be made progressively shallower through the first half of the maneuver and you should arrive at the crosswind point with a medium bank. This crosswind point will also be the position of maximum crab angle since the wind will be at your side and will be attempting to blow you away from the point. As your aircraft proceeds from the crosswind to the upwind position, your bank will be progressively shallowing out until you arrive at the upwind position with the most shallow bank of the entire maneuver. You will have now turned 180-degrees. At this point the entire banking procedure reverses and will get progressively steeper as you go from upwind to crosswind. Again at the crosswind point will be your maximum crab angle into the wind. Proceeding from crosswind, the bank continues to steepen until you arrive back at the downwind starting point and again have the steepest bank of the maneuver (Fig. 3-3).

It is probably best to practice turns-about-a-point in a steady breeze of from say 10 to 15 mph. This will give you the best opportunity to learn about the maneuver without having to overwork or underwork yourself. You see, a strong, gusty wind condition may cause you some difficulties in acquiring a feel for changes in your ground speed and resultant banks required to form a con-

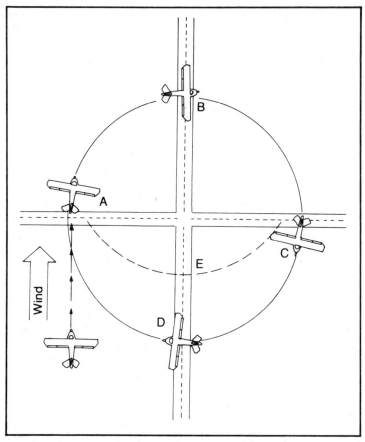

Fig. 3-3. Turn-about-a-point. (A) Enter downwind, fastest ground speed, steepest bank. (B) Crosswind point, maximum crab angle, medium bank. (C) Upwind point, slowest ground speed, shallow bank. (D) Crosswind point, maximum crab angle, medium bank. (E) Most common error, hurried turn from upwind, unequal symmetry results from the wind drifting aircraft back towards the road.

stant radius about the point. On the other hand, in a very calm wind your bank would be constant throughout the 360-degreee turn and nothing would be accomplished in regard to learning about differing banks in differing ground speed conditions. Also, strive to maintain a constant altitude throughout the maneuver.

S-TURNS

The S-turn is another good training maneuver requiring the same bank techniques incorporated in the turn-about-a-point. The

S-turn differs from the turn-about-a-point in that instead of turning a complete 360-degree circle, you will be making a series of 180-degree turns along a road. As with all ground reference maneuvers, your crab angle, along with your shallow, medium, and steep banks remain as your primary guides in obtaining the desired track over the ground.

The S-turn is begun at about 600 feet above any obstructions and over a road that lies perpendicular to the wind. You will want to enter downwind for the same reasons you do for the turn-about-a-point. As you approach the road heading downwind, decide how large you want your half-circles to be. Remember, the points of maximum distance from the road should be equidistant on both sides of the road. This equidistance will help you to maintain the desired symmetry of the maneuver.

The S-turn is begun when your aircraft is directly over the road. At this point your bank is initiated and will be the steepest of any in the maneuver because your ground speed will be your fastest. As you continue to the crosswind point, gradually shallow your bank to arrive at the crosswind point with a medium bank and your maximum crab angle into the wind. From crosswind, gradually shallow your bank even more as you get closer and closer to being directly upwind exactly over your road. At this point you will have the most shallow bank of the entire maneuver and your aircraft should be perpendicular to the road. You have now turned 180-degrees and have completed half of the S-turn.

As you cross over the road, upwind, reverse your bank for the turn in the opposite direction. Your aircraft is still upwind, so you begin with a shallow bank that will allow your aircraft to fly out away from the road, maintaining the symmetry of the maneuver. As you become nearer to crosswind, gradually steepen your bank so that you arrive at the crosswind point with a medium bank and, again, your maximum crab angle for this side of the maneuver.

From crosswind, continue to steepen your bank gradually until you arrive back over the road with your steepest bank for this half of the maneuver. You should arrive back over the road just as you complete the 180-degree turn, not before or after (Fig. 3-4).

The two half-circles you just completed form one complete S-turn. Of course, you should continue on down the road; you don't have to stop with just one S-turn. In fact, it's probably better practice for you to put together several in one direction and then reverse your course and go back down the road in the opposite direction. Be cautious and don't become so engrossed in your

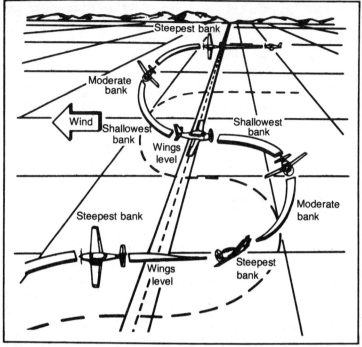

Fig. 3-4. S-turn. (courtesy FAA)

practice that you forget to watch for other aircraft. Seldom are you as alone as you think you are. In fact, I once watched as two aircraft did turns-about-a-point around the same point, neither apparently realizing the other was there. They looked like two vultures circling a dead cow. Be on the lookout.

The S-turn may be made any size you desire. The only thing governing the size of your half-circles is your initial bank. The steeper your initial bank, the smaller your circle will be. The shallower your initial bank, the larger your circle will be. And this is very important: The symmetry of your S-turn is kept uniform by going twice as far down the road as you go out from the road. If followed, this formula will ensure a perfect half-circle.

The list of common errors in the execution of S-turns, would be headed by the pilot hurrying his turn from upwind. At this point the ground speed is the slowest and there is a tendency to not hold the shallow bank long enough for the aircraft to fly away from the road as far as it was on the downwind side. The best way to overcome this is to pick two reference points of equal distance from both sides of the road and then, without cutting corners, fly to them.

Another common error is crossing the road before or after the maneuver is completed. You should cross the road just as the 180-degree turn is completed and then roll immediately into a turn in the opposite direction. Also, a brief glance at your altimeter every so often will enable you to maintain a better consistency with your altitude. Notice I said a *brief* glance. You don't want to stare at your altimeter because this maneuver requires the vast majority of your attention outside the cockpit.

I think the S-turn is one of the better coordination exercises because you have to use visual and instrument references, your feel for the aircraft's handling, and all your senses (with the possible exceptions of taste and smell). Also, while you are doing all this turning from one direction to the other, you must watch for other aircraft as well as monitor your headings, altitude, airspeed, and bank. This constant monitoring develops your ability to think and act quickly and accurately. If taken seriously, the S-turn is a very exacting and demanding maneuver. It will do much to help you learn precise coordination as you fly a given track over the ground.

RECTANGULAR PATTERNS

The rectangular pattern is another ground track maneuver that involves not only varying your bank to correct for wind drift, but also a great deal of crabbing into the wind. In the S-turn and the turn-about-a-point, there was little crabbing because the aircraft was in a turn throughout the entire maneuver. In this maneuver, however, there is a lot of straight and level flight with the crab as your only means of correcting for wind drift.

The rectangular pattern is flown parallel to, and equidistant from, the field or group of fields used to make up the rectangle. As in all ground track maneuvers, the entry is made downwind and your altitude will again be about 600 feet above obstructions.

Fly your aircraft to a point parallel to the downwind corner of the field; at this point, the maneuver is begun. The first portion of the maneuver will find you flying parallel to your field on a downwind heading. Remember, you will have to crab as necessary to maintain your distance from the field. At the downwind corner of the field you make your first turn. Since the turn is from downwind to crosswind, your bank will begin steep and then gradually shallow out to a medium bank as you reach the crosswind point. Your turn should be complete with all crab established at a point directly parallel to the corner of the field. This first turn will be more than 90 degrees because of the crab angle required to maintain a straight ground track. Continue on, crabbing to hold a constant distance from the downwind side of the field, until you reach a point directly parallel to the next corner of the field.

Upon reaching the second corner, you will still be crosswind, so your initial bank will be medium and will gradually decrease to shallow as you reach the point where you are into the wind and parallel to the corner of the field. This turn is less than 90 degrees because the turn was begun with your aircraft in a crabbed situation pointing slightly into the wind, and it ended up pointing directly upwind (into the wind). All of these points assume the wind was on your nose when you finished the previous turn. If it was not, crab as necessary to hold your distance constant from the field.

At the third corner, your aircraft is pointed into the wind so your initial bank will be shallow and gradually increase to medium as you reach the crosswind position. This turn will be less than 90 degrees since your turn was started pointing directly into the wind. The turn will finish up crosswind, however, requiring you to maintain a crab to hold your distance from the field constant.

Upon reaching a point parallel to the fourth corner (remember you are still crosswind), start out with a medium bank and gradually increase it to steep as you turn downwind. This turn will be more than 90 degrees because you started the turn with a crab into the wind and finished up in a directly downwind position. If you are directly downwind, no crab should be required to hold your path an equal distance from the field on this leg. You have no completed one circuit of a rectangular pattern (Fig. 3-5).

As you have probably surmised, the rectangular pattern has a direct relationship to the normal traffic pattern. Since all really good traffic patterns are rectangular, it is important that you understand how this maneuver transfers to the traffic pattern. I have seen many pilots who have gone to all the trouble to learn how to execute a good rectangular pattern and then forget they ever saw or heard of it when they enter the traffic pattern. They fail to allow for the wind and proceed to fly some very erratic patterns. This is a prime example of learning a specific maneuver and then not using it in a practical situation.

I have had students who, after an entire flight period of dual on the importance of ground tracking, have entered the traffic pattern and been blown so far off course that I have given serious thought to becoming an ax murderer. They simply do not apply the basic technique learned during the lesson to the situation at hand. To an instructor, this is extremely frustrating. The problem is that you

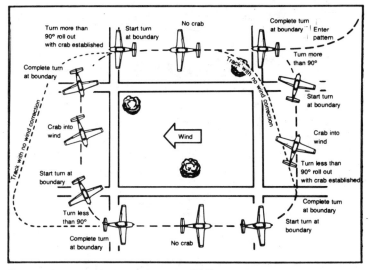

Fig. 3-5. Rectangular pattern. (courtesy FAA)

can teach a person how to do a certain maneuver, but you can't teach him how to *think*.

No matter how well you can execute a maneuver out in the practice area, you must be able to translate this learning to a real-life situation. Only then may you be sure that true learning has taken place. Instructors do not teach you all these maneuvers simply to give an examiner something to look at during a check ride. They must be *learned, remembered,* and *put to use* throughout your flying career. They must become habits.

Having been a pilot for 20 years, a flight instructor for 17 years, and also an FAA Designated Pilot Examiner and Accident Prevention Counselor, I can tell you from experience that one of the foremost problems with pilot technique is failure to allow and compensate for varying wind conditions. This causes more accidents than almost any other flight operation (and this would include all phases from taxi to cross-country flying). If you have any doubts about your ability to handle any given wind situation, find a good instructor and get some dual to help iron out the rough spots. Believe me, it will pay off in many ways.

Chapter 4

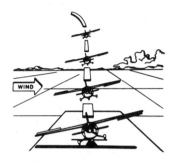

Advanced Maneuvers

Now that we have covered the basics and ground track maneuvers, let's proceed with some advanced maneuvers. As you begin your practice of advanced maneuvers, remember that *all* flight is made up of the four basic fundamentals. You will still be relying on your old friends straight and level, climbs, turns, and glides. You will merely be using them in a little different sequence than you have been used to.

CHANDELLE

A chandelle is nothing more than an advanced maneuver that incorporates three of the basics (straight and level, climbs, and turns) into a composite maneuver—a 180-degree climbing turn. In order to correctly execute a chandelle, a great deal of planning, coordination, and timing are required on your part. With a little practice, however, you should have no problem mastering this advanced maneuver.

The chandelle is usually begun at least 1500 feet above the ground to allow sufficient altitude for recovery in the event you should happen to stall out of the maneuver. (And if you happen to stall while performing a chandelle, merely put to good use the stall recovery techniques you have already learned.)

Next, you will need to pick at least three visual reference points to complete the chandelle using outside visual references. You will need one reference point directly ahead of you, one at the

90-degree point, and one at the 180-degree point where the maneuver will be completed. Since you don't want to be blown out of your practice area, begin the chandelle crosswind and make all of your turns into the wind. There seems to be some erroneous thinking on the part of some students as to what is meant by starting the maneuver crosswind. Simply put, you just figure out where the wind is coming from and turn so that it is off your wing tip—this is crosswind and you are ready to begin your chandelle. When you are through, the wind will be on the opposite side of your aircraft. You will have turned 180-degrees.

When you are crosswind, with your three reference points and at maneuvering speed for your particular aircraft, you are ready to begin. Roll into a moderate bank and then begin to increase your pitch smoothly. The pitch will be steadily increased until you reach the highest point of pitch at the 90-degree point of the turn. Somewhere about the 45-degree point you will have to add some right rudder to help correct the left-turning tendency caused by torque and P-factor. This application of right rudder, in turns in both directions, will also help in making the turns both equal in rate of turn, which is very important if you want to make the chandelle precise in both left and right turns.

Upon reaching the 90-degree point, maintain a constant pitch attitude and begin rolling out of the bank proportional to your rate of turn. Continue to correct for the effects of torque and P-factor with your right rudder. The rollout should be timed so that as you arrive at the 180 degree point, the wings will just be coming level and your

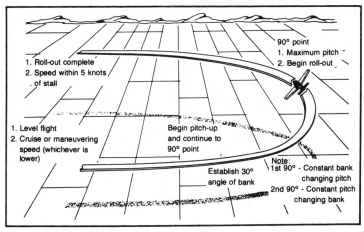

Fig. 4-1. Chandelle. (courtesy FAA)

airspeed should be just above a stall (Fig. 4-1). *Note:* Any pitch change after reaching the 90-degree point is evidence of improper planning.

To maintain a constant pitch attitude, bring the elevator control back slightly while you are turning from the 90 to the 180-degree point to compensate for your loss of airspeed and the resultant control ineffectiveness.

The most common mistake made in executing the chandelle (other than the obvious pitch and bank errors) is a tendency for many pilots to hurry the maneuver. I think you will find that chandelles done as slowly and smoothly as possible are usually the best. This will result in the greatest gain of altitude, and, more importantly, help you to feel the vast difference in control effectiveness as your aircraft slows from maneuvering speed down to just above a stall. Also, watch for that torque and P-factor correction mentioned previously. Proper correction will go a long way in helping your chandelles to become meaningful and precise.

It's not the quantity of altitude you gain while performing your chandelle that is important; it's the quality of your technique that really counts.

LAZY-8

The lazy-8 is another advanced training maneuver requiring planning, coordination, and timing. One interesting aspect of the lazy-8 is that there are almost as many ways of performing a lazy-8 as there are pilots. Once common denominator emerges: The lazy-8 is a superb training maneuver for everyone. The lazy-8 can also be unequalled in frustration and anxiety for those who don't understand the various aspects of this complex maneuver. I believe the lazy-8 is really a fairly simple maneuver if you are well-schooled in your basic coordination techniques and the use of outside visual references.

To begin your practice of lazy-8s, align your aircraft crosswind as you did for the chandelle. For the same reasons as the chandelle, all turns are made into the wind.

Five outside visual reference points are needed to help you complete a precise lazy-8. These reference points will have to be on the horizon directly ahead of your aircraft and at each 45-degrees of turn. In other words, the five reference points will begin with the first directly ahead and one each at the 45, 90, 135, and 180-degree points.

A well-executed lazy-8 is begun and ended at the same altitude and airspeed. For this reason, power selection is an important factor in a well-executed lazy-8. You don't want too much power, which can cause you to gain more altitude than you can comfortably lose. On the other hand, too little power can cause too little altitude gain and destroy the symmetry of the maneuver. It is also important to begin a lazy-8 at or below maneuvering speed.

Unlike the chandelle, in which you had to begin your roll first and *then* initiate the pitch-up, the lazy-8 calls for a simultaneous initiation of both pitch and bank. The pitch and bank are begun slowly. Remember the name: *lazy-8*. It's not an accelerated-8 or an abrupt-8; it's a *lazy*-8.

Slowly and smoothly begin the pitch and bank simultaneously. The pitch and bank are continuously increased, slowly, until your aircraft arrives at the 45-degree point of your turn just as the highest pitch is reached and your bank is arriving at about 15-degrees. At this time, due to the very slow airspeed and high angle of attack, continued application of the bank will cause your aircraft to lose some of its vertical lift. The aircraft will then fly down through the horizon at the 90-degree point of the turn as your bank reaches the 30-degree point.

As you pass through the 90-degree point, some back pressure is released and your bank is reversed so you arrive at the 135-degree point with your bank back to about 15-degrees again and your nose as much below the horizon as it was above it at the 45-degree point. The purpose of the nose being as much below the horizon as it was above it is to achieve maximum symmetry.

From the 135-degree point, continue to slowly reduce the bank and adjust your pitch so that you arrive at the 180-degree point just as the wings come level and your airspeed and altitude return to their initial starting point. To complete the lazy-8, follow the same procedure in the opposite direction. Remember, it takes two 180 degree turns to properly complete a lazy-8 (Fig. 4-2).

Your timing and coordination are important to the symmetry of the lazy-8. At no time during the maneuver will your controls be held constant. The pitch and bank are constantly changing during the climbing and descending turns, and corrections for torque and P-factor are needed during the climbing portions of the maneuver. This leads to a cross-controlled situation in the climbing left turn since the bank is continuously increasing to the left. If right rudder is added to aid in overcoming torque (or no correction is made) then a situation is set up where you are either cross-controlled and coordinated or, in the second instance, in a slipping turn.

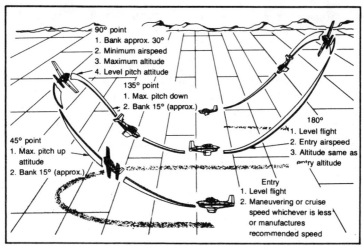

90° point
1. Bank approx. 30°
2. Minimum airspeed
3. Maximum altitude
4. Level pitch attitude

135° point
1. Max. pitch down
2. Bank 15° (approx.)

180°
1. Level flight
2. Entry airspeed
3. Altitude same as entry altitude

45° point
1. Max. pitch up attitude
2. Bank 15° (approx.)

Entry
1. Level flight
2. Maneuvering or cruise speed whichever is less or manufactures recommended speed

Fig. 4-2. Lazy-8. (courtesy FAA)

There are three distinct errors common while learning to execute a lazy-8. The most common is to hurry the maneuver. As mentioned previously, it is not called an accelerated-8, it should be done slowly and smoothly for the best outcome.

The second most common error is for the longitudinal axis of the aircraft to pass through the horizon either too early or too late. It should fly through the horizon at exactly the 90-degree point. If the longitudinal axis passes through the horizon too early, you will usually complete the lazy-8 at an altitude lower than that at which you entered. This is because passing through the horizon early gives the aircraft more time to descend and it winds up using this time to descend more than it climbed, thus destroying the symmetry of the maneuver. Conversely, if the longitudinal axis passes through the horizon late, the maneuver will be completed at an altitude higher than the original. The reason for this is just the opposite of passing through the horizon too early. The aircraft will not have as much time in which to descend and this causes the maneuver to end up at an altitude higher than which it started. Now, you may cheat and force your aircraft to return to its original altitude, but the symmetry is destroyed and you will make little gain in understanding the precision involved in mastering the maneuver.

The third most common error concerns power selection. The correct power setting is essential if the lazy-8 is to be performed with any degree of symmetry. For example, the power setting you choose on a day when you are the only person on board, with half fuel and a 35-degree outside air temperature, will be quite different than if you are dual and have full fuel on a very hot day. The reasoning behind this involves your density altitude and power-to-weight ratio. The lighter your aircraft is on a cool day, the less power you will need to make the lazy-8 symmetrical. Simply put, when the air is cool and you are light, if you use too much power you will gain more altitude than you can comfortably lose in the descent portion of the lazy-8. This will usually cause you to wind up higher at the end of the maneuver than you were at the beginning. On the other hand, if you select too little power for a given day, you will not climb enough to make your lazy-8 symmetrical. So before you initiate your lazy-8, do yourself a big favor and give some serious thought to what power setting should be right for the conditions you have on this particular day. Don't merely try to use the same old power settings day in and day out. It won't work.

Chapter 5

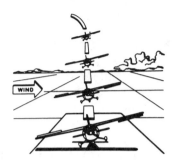

Takeoffs and Landings

To many new pilots, the takeoff and the landing seem to be the sum total of aviation. These types seem to feel that they can demonstrate their proficiency as pilots by their mastery of the normal takeoff and landing. There are *many* things that lead to good, precise, piloting ability. Takeoffs and landings are but two of the pieces of a much larger overall picture of precision flight. Granted, the takeoff and the landing are important, but to do so with great skill, confidence, and precision you must first master a host of other important and related tasks. When these basic tasks are mastered, then you are ready for work in the traffic pattern, but not before.

NORMAL OPERATIONS

With today's modern tricycle gear aircraft and miles and miles of hard-surfaced runways, the normal takeoff is one of the easiest maneuvers to master. All you have to do is point your aircraft straight down the runway, apply power, keep it straight until you reach rotation speed, and pull back a little on the yoke. It's that simple. Or is it? If you are a robot, it is. If you want to become a precision pilot, there's a little more involved. Part of this involvement includes how your control effectiveness increases as your speed increases and how you might go about straightening out a takeoff that has begun to go astray. Or you might want to think about how you are going to keep an eye on your runway alignment, airspeed indicator, and oil pressure, all at the same time. If you stop and think about all the factors that go into a really precise normal takeoff, I believe you will find there are a good many procedures that you just cannot take for granted.

Normal Takeoff

If you have learned your lessons well out in the practice area pertaining to all the basics—slow flight, stalls, and all the rest— then the normal takeoff should hold few surprises for you. If not— well, you had better go back out and drill until they become ingrained habits or you will probably find normal takeoffs more difficult than you imagined. You *are* ready to go, aren't you? You have carefully preflighted your aircraft, completed the run-up, taxied to but not onto the active runway, double-checked the fuel, mixture, oil pressure, carb heat, primer locked, flaps as required, and cleared the area for any other traffic, haven't you? If so, then you are ready to go.

Pull onto the runway at the end. Don't waste a hundred yards of that precious material weaving back and forth to line up with the centerline; go right to it. Remember, any runway behind you may as well be in another country. It is of no use to you. Line up your longitudinal axis (nose to tail axis) with the runway centerline and smoothly add full power. You will probably need to add a little right rudder as you feed in your power to overcome the left-turning tendency of torque. Notice how your controls begin to come alive as you gather airspeed. Glance quickly at your oil pressure and airspeed indicator, then get your eyes back out where the action is. If you stare too long at your instruments, there may be more action waiting for you out there than you had anticipated. Quick glances back into the cockpit to check airspeed should be all that is needed once you have reached full power and are accelerating.

As your aircraft gains speed and your controls become more effective, use only small control inputs to maintain your alignment straight down the runway. One of the most common mistakes made by low-time pilots is to overcontrol—especially the rudder—during the takeoff run. Do not, however, go the other way and be too timid with the controls. Use as much control input as you need—no more, no less.

When you reach rotation speed for your aircraft, apply a smooth back pressure and lift off (Fig. 5-1). Your aircraft should be rotated so that you will be at an angle that will produce a climb at about V_y (best rate of climb speed). If you find this a little difficult at first, don't feel alone. Learning to rotate to the proper angle will

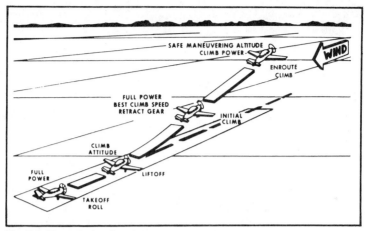

Fig. 5-1. Normal takeoff and climb. (courtesy FAA)

come with time and practice. Here again, it is best to use too little than too much control input, but strive to reach the point where you use the exact amount of back pressure for liftoff.

Now you're airborne and climbing out at V_y. Trim your aircraft to help you to maintain that airspeed and take a quick glance around to be sure that you are climbing straight out from the runway centerline. Correct any drifting tendency you might encounter with the crab method (Fig. 5-2). Remember, you learned to correct for

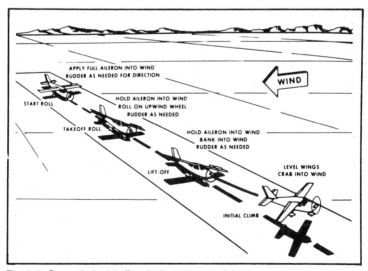

Fig. 5-2. Crosswind takeoff and climb. (courtesy FAA)

wind back when you learned ground track procedures; now is a good time to put that knowledge to practical use.

The FAA recommends climbing out to at least 400 feet above the ground before turning to leave the traffic pattern. Another good suggestion is to climb straight on the runway heading until you have reached the end of the runway. I believe a combination of the two will bring the best and safest results. Unless you are directed otherwise, climb to at least 400 feet, or to the end of the runway, whichever comes *last*. The main reasoning behind this is to try for better standardization from one airport to another. It will also make your departure safer and more precise.

Normal Landing

There's an old axiom in aviation that states "A good landing is usually preceded by a good approach." And this statement is just as true now as it ever was. A normal landing, the one you learn before going on to master the other, more difficult types, is really much akin to the other landings. It is merely the end result of a period in which you make a transition from your normal approach attitude, through level flight attitude, into the nose-high flare, and to ultimate ground contact.

There are only two options you have open to you regarding ground contact. You may either *land* or you may *arrive*. Arrivals are usually very funny to watch. Your friends will love to rush up to you and tell you of your arrival. Words often heard in association with arrivals are *pranged, bent, dropped,* and *flat tire*—not good for your ego. Landings, on the other hand, are just the opposite of arrivals. A landing is usually smooth and controlled. Your best bet is to land.

A normal landing begins long before the actual ground contact. It starts with your planning for your pattern (Fig. 5-3), airspeed, traffic spacing, flap usage, and all the other basic flight techniques you have previously learned. The FAA has a good saying: "A good landing is no accident." And this is true in more ways than one.

On the downwind leg, go through your pre-landing checklist, set up your aircraft at the proper distance from the runway, check for other traffic, and be sure that you are at traffic pattern altitude. I say again: *At* traffic pattern altitude, not just close to it. About halfway down the runway on your downwind leg, pull on your carb heat so it will have enough time to work effectively. Remember, the heat from the exhaust warms your carburetor when you pull on the carb heat and this heat is not exactly of blowtorch temperature—and even a blowtorch takes *some* time to melt ice.

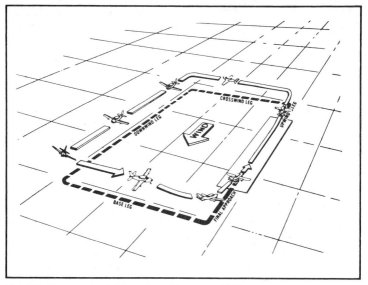

Fig. 5-3. Rectangular traffic pattern. (courtesy FAA)

Give your carb heat time enough to do its work.

When you are directly abeam of your point of intended landing, reduce your power to an approach setting and trim your aircraft to maintain your recommended approach speed. After you have set up your glide and your airspeed is in the white arc on the airspeed indicator (flap operating range), lower your first 10 degrees of flap and retrim the aircraft as necessary to maintain a constant approach speed.

Now comes one of the most important decisions you will have to make to keep your traffic pattern uniform: Just when should you turn from the downwind leg onto the base leg? A good rule of thumb is to turn from downwind to base as soon as there is a 45-degree angle running from the end of the runway to a point at the rear of the wing nearest the runway. This procedure prevents you from developing the bad habit of turning when you are over a certain tree, house, barn, etc. You see, if you develop the habit of turning base when you arrive over a certain ground reference point, that reference point probably won't be there at another airport. You will always have a runway end and your wing tip with you, so by learning this method you should be able to fly a pretty uniform traffic pattern no matter how unfamiliar you are with the airport.

On base leg we find the point in the traffic pattern called the *key position*. It is the position in the pattern reserved for another important decision: Are you too high, too low, or just right? If you are anything other than just right, this is the time to start making some corrections. If you are just right, add another 10 degrees of flap, retrim as necessary, and continue on. Use your power as you need it—that's why the throttle moves. You will find that small power changes, introduced at the proper time, will do more to smooth out your approach than large changes made too late. In short, don't be timid with the power.

Let's try to answer one of the most frequently asked questions about the traffic pattern. What should you do if you are too high or too low? The answer is about 50 percent common sense, 48 percent experience, and 2 percent instruction. Since there are about ten thousand different possibilities of combinations of errors, I will try to give you some general pointers.

If you are approaching with constant power, constant airspeed, full flaps and are getting too low, the first thing to do is to add some power; this should alleviate the problem. Merely fly your aircraft up to the point where you reintercept the glide path, reduce your power back to your approach setting, and continue on to land. If a little power doesn't work, try a lot. Use it as you need it. That's what it's there for. I personally find it much preferable to add a lot of power and land on the runway than maintain a beautiful glide, with the airspeed and attitude constant, and stick it in the mud. It's hard to taxi that way.

If you find yourself too high, there are many things you can do to alleviate the situation. Most pilots don't have too much trouble deciding what to do if they are too low. I guess it's the ground rushing up at them that stirs them into action. When some pilots are too high, however, it's an entirely different matter. They just sit there. I guess they figure they will come down sometime—and they will, probably in an orchard or a housing complex. There is every bit as much reason to act if you find yourself about to overshoot the runway as there is if you are too low. If you don't put your aircraft on the runway, the results are usually the same for you—trouble.

If you are too high and have not yet put down all of your flaps, you could add some more flap and increase your rate of descent. Or you could opt to reduce some, or even all, of your power. Perhaps you will need to do both in order to obtain a descent that will put you in a position from which a normal landing is practical (Fig. 5-4).

Yet another option (which I will discuss in more detail later) is the *slip*. A moderate forward slip can increase your sink rate a great deal and turn a possible go-around into a workable approach. I teach

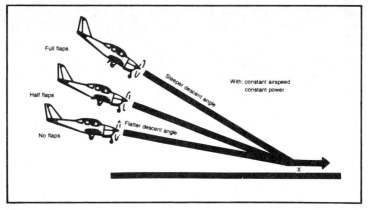

Fig. 5-4. The configuration of the aircraft will dictate the angle of final approach. (courtesy FAA)

my students all three methods and have them utilize them in the same order as just discussed. If they are high, they add some flaps. If they are still too high, they reduce some power. If that doesn't work, they slip it. Of course, if you see that you are still going to overshoot, nothing replaces the go-around, try-it-again method. In any case, don't just sit there and wait to see what happens; take some definite action.

Back on base leg, we left ourselves in the key position with 20-degrees of flap and normal approach speed. Your next step is to start your turn to final early enough so that you won't get caught having to steepen the turn to the point where you have a very steep bank (Fig. 5-5). You don't want this in the traffic pattern; moderate banks, at the most, should be used in the traffic pattern.

The opposite of the steep-banked procedure occurs when the pilot starts his turn from base to final too late, doesn't steepen the bank at all, and then uses what I call the *cotter-pin approach*. He overshoots the runway centerline and then has to turn back to reintercept it. Viewed from above, the flight path looks very much like a cotter pin. It also shows that the pilot has his head up and locked.

The easy solution to this real and present problem is to plan ahead and start your turn from base to final early enough to use the ground track procedures you learned earlier in your training. By starting your turn earlier, you'll wind up with an ever-decreasing bank as you reach your final approach course. I think you'll find this much easier than doing S-turns on final and hunting for the runway centerline.

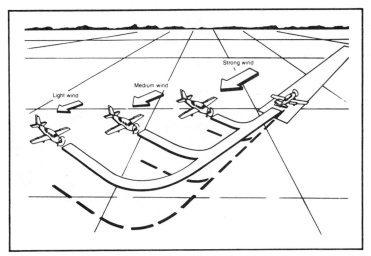

Fig. 5-5. A precise pilot will adjust the traffic pattern to allow for varying wind velocities. (courtesy FAA)

On final, keep your aircraft aligned with the runway centerline and add the remainder of your flaps as you need them. Maintain a constant airspeed and attitude. Your power is reduced as you no longer need it until, if all goes well, you reduce the power to idle in the landing flare (Figs. 5-6 through 5-8).

Fig. 5-6. A normal approach as seen from the cockpit. Right down the centerline.

Fig. 5-7. On down final. Whoops! A little wind gust. Continue on and fly it in.

Fig. 5-8. Short final. Everything looks good. The aircraft is lined up and ready to initiate the flare in a few moments.

If you have the approach pattern down pat, your landing should come rather easily. As I said before, the landing is merely a transition from the normal approach attitude to the attitude of touchdown. This transition usually begins about 15 to 20 feet above the runway with you *slowly* increasing your back pressure as you continue to sink. If you have too much airspeed or you pull back too rapidly, you will possibly climb a little. You don't want to do that, so increase your back pressure gradually. Although it may sound like a contradiction, in a normal landing, you almost think of it as trying to hold your aircraft off the ground as you increase the back pressure to arrive at your normal landing attitude. You are transitioning the aircraft from a nose-low approach attitude through level flight to a slightly nose-high attitude at touchdown.

If you have everything set up just right, you will reach the point where you run out of back pressure just an instant before your touchdown occurs on the main wheels. Since you land with your nose high, your nose gear will still be up off the runway at the moment of touchdown. As your speed decreases following the touchdown, allow the nose gear to lower and contact the runway, thus providing you with more positive directional control during the rollout (Figs. 5-9, 5-10).

Your landing is far from complete merely because you are on the ground. Many aircraft accidents occur during the rollout after touchdown. Keep your eyes outside the cockpit, making sure you are maintaining runway centerline during the slow-down process. Turn off the carb heat and bring up your flaps *after* you have cleared the active runway and are positive everything is under control. More than one beautiful landing has been spoiled by the pilot fumbling with something inside the cockpit too soon after

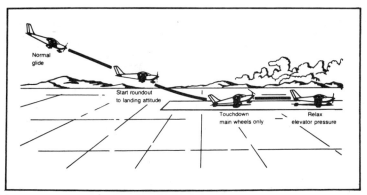

Fig. 5-9. Profile of a normal approach, flare, and touchdown. (courtesy FAA)

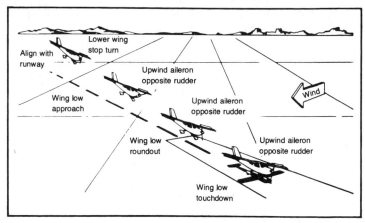

Fig. 5-10. Crosswind approach and touchdown. Keep the upwind wing low throughout the approach with enough opposite rudder to keep the aircraft aligned with the runway centerline. (courtesy FAA)

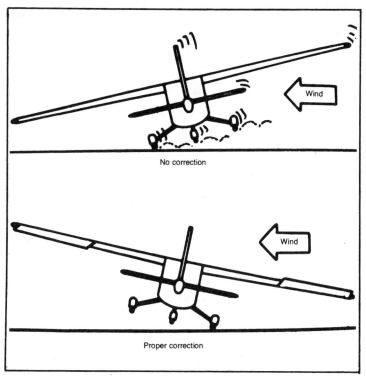

Fig. 5-11. Failure to apply correct crosswind correction can allow the wind to get under the upwind wing and create a potentially dangerous situation. (courtesy FAA)

touchdown. Sometimes the result of this inattention is a rude awakening by the sound of runway lights shattering as the aircraft wanders off the runway. Remember, your control effectiveness will decrease as your speed decreases. The slower you go, the more control movement it will take to get the job done (Fig. 5-11). Use care, but don't overcontrol in this stage of your landing. Use whatever control input is necessary—no more and no less.

Most of the errors common to normal landings (outside of a poor traffic pattern) have to do with visual reference points. Nobody can show you exactly where to look, but you can gain some insights by knowing where *not* to look:

☐ Do not look down and to the side while landing. Speed blurs your vision and you will not be able to tell whether you are five feet or five inches above the runway by looking down and to the side.

☐ Don't look too close in front of your aircraft during the landing flare (Fig. 5-12). Pilots who do this have a tendency to flare too high, stall, and drop in. This is not a pleasant way to land.

☐ Don't look too far ahead of your aircraft during the landing

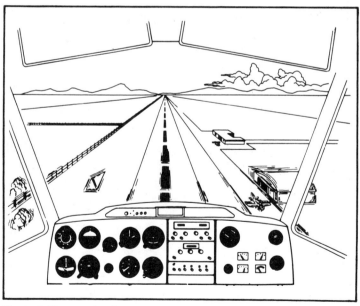

Fig. 5-12. The speed on final can blur your vision if you look too close in front of the aircraft. (courtesy FAA)

flare. Once again, due to depth perception, this causes many pilots to run their aircraft into the ground with little or no flare. This, too, is not fun.

☐ Once you are into your landing flare, don't look inside the cockpit for any reason. You've got to see where you are going.

Now that I have told you where not to look, am I going to tell you where to look? No, but I am going to show you a method to try so you may attempt to figure out for yourself where to look during the landing flare. During the short final and flare-out, look approximately as far ahead of your aircraft as you would look if you were in a car traveling at the same rate of speed. This should be something that you can visualize and something to compare with. (If you do not drive, I guess it's trial and error.)

One other very common error associated with learning to land is not pulling the yoke *straight* back. I have had students who would begin to flare perfectly, and then about 10 feet up, turn and try and take it to the tiedown area. The problem lies in flare technique. In most aircraft, the flare requires the coordinated use of your hand, wrist, elbow, and shoulder. If you try to flare using only your hand, wrist, and elbow but not including your shoulder, the tendency will be to twist your elbow up and out, causing your ailerons to be deflected to the right. This in turn will cause a right turn tendency that may spoil an otherwise decent approach and flare. If you have problems in this area, I suggest that you sit in your aircraft and practice pulling the yoke *straight* back—no kidding.

SLIPS

Have you ever heard of a *slip*? Have you ever tried one? It seems to me that slips-to-a-landing are going the route of spins. Not too many people pay much attention to them anymore. I guess the advent of flaps and spoilers has caused slip training to be pushed to the rear on the list of things a pilot should learn; however, they still have a very real place in the mind of a precise pilot.

The comments I keep hearing sound like this: "If you have flaps you don't need to slip; and anyway, it's unsafe to slip with your flaps down." To this I politely say, "nonsense." Unless your particular aircraft is placarded against slipping with flaps, go ahead and slip it. Even the aircraft that are placarded concerning slipping with flaps down don't always prohibit slips. They usually say: "Avoid slipping with flaps extended." *Avoid* is the key word here—it doesn't say *prohibited.* If your aircraft is prohibited from slipping with flaps, don't. Otherwise, why not? Slipping with your flaps down just might get you into a landing area that you might have otherwise overshot. This could be especially true in an emergency situation. I for one am not going to sit there and watch the world slide by, waiting patiently for the trees to gather me up into so much useless aluminum and flesh, if I can slip my aircraft down into a nice, smooth, landing area.

For those of you who are not going to slip no matter what, skip this part. Better still, read it. It just might change your thinking and help you to become a more precise pilot. And it really could save your life—literally.

Generally, there are but two varieties of the slip: The *forward slip* and the *side slip* (Fig. 5-13). Although the two are very much alike in the manner in which they are executed, the forward slip usually requires much larger doses of control input. The one facet in which both are alike is the fact that you have to have your controls crossed in order to maintain a slip. You will be holding your ailerons in one direction and your rudder in the other, which is something many pilots find rather uncomfortable until they have executed many slips. If you have any wind, the slip should be done into the

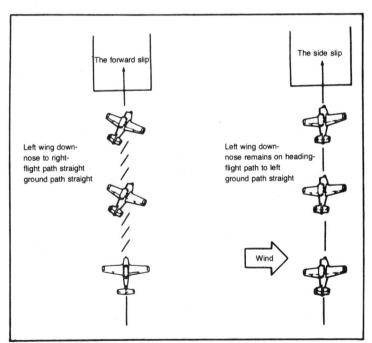

Fig. 5-13. The forward slip and the side slip. (courtesy FAA)

wind. That is, if the wind is coming from your left, the left wing is the one that is lowered. But if all you do is lower your left wing, what will happen? You'll turn left, won't you? To keep your aircraft from turning, you have to add opposite rudder. Now you are cross-controlled—in other words, slipping.

In order to put these slips to work for you, you need to know what each one is used for and what the desired results will be. The forward slip is used mainly for altitude loss. The side slip is used to align your aircraft with the runway and for touchdown in a crosswind.

The Forward Slip

Let's set up a situation where you will have to use both types of slips on one final approach and landing. Let's say you have turned from base leg to final approach and find yourself very high. A crosswind will complete our example; you are landing on runway 18 and the wind is from 120 degrees at 10 knots. You already have full flaps and your power is at idle, yet you are still going to overshoot. Now what? If you are very high, you would be wise to go around. If you are only a little too high, however, the forward slip just might get you onto that runway safely.

Lower your wing into the wind as you add opposite rudder. In this case, you lower your left wing and add some right rudder. You want the nose of your aircraft to swing past direct runway alignment—say, 15 to 20 degrees to the right. You will still be tracking straight down the runway, but your nose will be pointing to a heading of 200 degrees or so. Now comes the important part: Don't let your airspeed build up much over your normal approach speed. If you do, all the gain you will be getting from the slip will be lost because the increased airspeed will cause you to float much farther down the runway while you are bleeding off that airspeed.

Continue to slip until you are down to the point where you reintercept your normal glide path and then get out of the slip and continue with your approach. How do you get out of a slip? You get out of a a a slip by reversing your ailerons and rudder, bringing your aircraft back to level flight with the ailerons and using your left rudder to swing the nose back to direct runway alignment or proba-bly a little past. Most likely, since you have a crosswind, you continue to bring your nose back past direct runway alignment into a crab condition in order to take care of the crosswind. Now you will have lost the unwanted altitude, will still be tracking straight down the runway, and will be ready to complete a normal crosswind landing.

Remember, in a forward slip your aircraft is traveling over the ground in one direction but pointing in another. Your longitudinal axis will *not* be aligned with your flight path. Also, this slip is used primarily for altitude loss and is valuable in losing unwanted altitude without an increase in your airspeed. Try it. You just might find an alternative method of altitude loss in addition to flaps.

The Side Slip

The best use for the side slip is in the performance of a crosswind landing (Fig. 5-14). In the side slip, the longitudinal axis of your aircraft remains parallel to the flight path. Since you don't want to land in a crab (unless you are into the sounds of tires squealing and aluminum twisting), you have to find a way to get your aircraft straight down the runway before you touch down. The side slip is, I believe, the best answer.

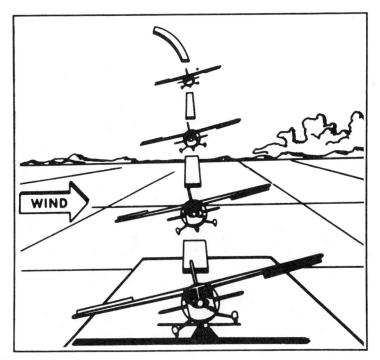

Fig. 5-14. The side slip as used for an approach and landing in a crosswind. (courtesy FAA)

In the side slip, you lower your wing into the wind and add opposite rudder as you did in the forward slip, but you add only enough rudder to maintain your track straight down the runway. You are sort of leaning into the wind, just as you did back when you rode your bicycle in a strong crosswind. You still go in a straight line, but are banked to correct for the crosswind (Figs. 5-15 through 5-17). It usually takes a little time before a pilot becomes comfortable in the use of the side slip since landing with a wing held down is rather different from the methods learned earlier in landing practice. It also requires a good bit of practice before most pilots really master the side slip and crosswind landing. Usually, you will not be able to put your wing down x number of degrees and leave it there because the wind will most likely play its usual tricks, increasing and decreasing in intensity, forcing you to make rapid control changes to compensate. The main thing is to keep your aircraft aligned straight down the centerline and don't let it wander. Use whatever it takes to maintain your runway alignment before, during, and after touchdown.

The crosswind landing is accomplished exactly as any other landing, except you have to keep your side slip throughout your

Fig. 5-15. A side slip approach as viewed from the cockpit. Wing down into the wind, runway centered, and airspeed constant.

Fig. 5-16. Getting closer in, keep the wing down into the wind and the runway aligned with the longitudinal axis.

Fig. 5-17. Maintain the side slip throughout the remainder of the approach and crosswind touchdown.

approach, flare, and actual touchdown. And remember, after your touchdown, you're not through yet. Maintain your upwind wing down into the wind and use your rudders as needed to maintain your runway heading. As you slow down, add more aileron into the wind since your controls become less and less effective as your speed slows. In fact, as you reach your slowest speed, you will want *full* aileron deflection into the wind to correct for the crosswind just as if you were taxiing. By the way, that *is* taxiing.

SOFT-FIELD OPERATIONS

Soft-field takeoffs and landings are useful to all pilots. Their techniques are used to get into or out of not only soft fields, but also rough fields, deep snow, and tall grass. In fact, they are used almost anytime you are not using a smooth, hard-surfaced runway. Your primary concern is to prevent the aircraft from nosing over during the takeoff run or the landing roll.

Soft-Field Takeoff

For a soft-field takeoff, set your flaps as per the manufacturer's recommended flap setting if your aircraft is so equipped. (Many low-wing aircraft manufacturers recommend using *no* flaps in a soft-field condition, since the flaps are very close to the ground and can be easily damaged by mud, rocks, etc.) Since the surface is soft, it is important that once you start your aircraft moving, you *keep* it moving. Even taxiing should be done with full aft yoke to help prevent any tendency the aircraft may have to try to nose over.

In the soft-field takeoff, your first concern is to transfer the weight of the aircraft from the wheels to the wings as rapidly as possible. The flaps will help in this respect, but at the start of the soft-field takeoff run you should have your yoke full back to help bring the nosewheel out of the impeding substance as rapidly as possible and to help reduce the parasitic drag caused by the soft surface. This will give you an angle of attack much higher than you are used to, so care must be taken to see that once the nose *does* begin to come up, you relax a bit of your back pressure so you don't wind up smacking your tail into the ground. It is easy to hold too much back pressure and over-pitch your aircraft, causing a tail strike. This usually scares a pilot into the mistake of shoving the nose forward—sometimes a little too far. The result is often sticking your nosewheel back into the soft surface even deeper than it was at the start of the takeoff run. This sort of stick-jockeying can lead to a very nasty noseover—exactly the thing you are trying to

68

avoid. Know that this can happen and watch for it.

Once you have your nose at the desired attitude and are rolling down the runway, keep your nose attitude constant until the aircraft flies itself off of the ground. The liftoff should occur at a much lower than normal airspeed because of the high angle of attack. For this reason, once the aircraft becomes airborne, the angle of attack must be slowly and smoothly reduced to near the level flight attitude as the aircraft accelerates toward normal climb speed. You should maintain this near-level flight attitude, remaining in ground effect, until you reach your normal climb speed. This speed will be either V_x or V_y depending on whether or not there is an obstruction to be cleared.

After you have accelerated in ground effect to your desired speed, start a normal climbout and bring your flaps up after you are *sure* you are maintaining a climb. Don't be in a hurry to bring up your flaps; they are providing lift and bringing them up too soon could cause a momentary sink that might prove undesirable.

One other important point concerning soft-field takeoffs (or *any* takeoff, for that matter) is to be very sure that you lift off and maintain a straight track down the runway. If you have a crosswind, you may have the tendency to crab into the wind as soon as you lift off. If you should settle back onto the runway in this crabbed condition, the result will most likely be one of the shortest and most dismal flights you will ever have. At the very least you will test the integrity of your tires and landing gear. Use the wing-low side-slip method discussed earlier for crosswind takeoffs and landings. After liftoff, keep your aircraft in this side slip while heading straight down the runway until you are positive that you are going to remain in the air in a stable climb.

Soft-Field Landing

Your approach to the soft-field landing should be made at normal approach speed. The touchdown should be at as slow an airspeed as possible in order to minimize the noseover tendency. Unless you are in a low-wing aircraft and the manufacturer recommends no-flap landings in a soft field, this usually means an approach and landing using full flaps. The touchdown should be with flaps as recommended, full stall, and full back stick (Fig. 5-18). A small amount of power may be used during the flare to help bring your nose up and to provide momentum, which will be very helpful in the prevention of the noseover tendency.

Keep your stick in the full back position during the rollout and

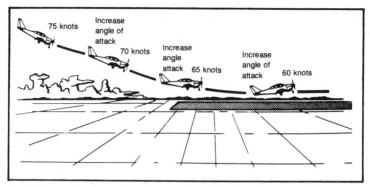

Fig. 5-18. Profile of a soft-field approach and landing. (courtesy FAA)

be ready to use power to help you get through any really soft spots such as snow drifts, mud, and so on. When you are safely on firm ground and slow enough to taxi, you may then get your carb heat off and retract your flaps. Use caution as you taxi; you could still hit some soft spots or drifted snow and wind up mired down a goodly ways from the tiedown area. Remember, you haven't got it made until you are putting the ropes on it.

The list of common errors committed during the soft-field approach and landing would include poor airspeed control and landing with less than full back stick. Time and time again I have seen pilots make a practice soft-field landing that is feather-soft but without full back stick upon touchdown. Doing this is the same as inviting the Welcome Wagon to a noseover party. Keep your stick full aft during touchdown (Fig. 5-19).

SHORT-FIELD OPERATIONS

The short-field takeoff and landing may be required to get you into or out of fields that are measurably shorter than the ones you are probably used to. Even though the runway may be as long as the one you normally use, the possibility exists of some type of obstruction that could shorten the effective runway length. The effective runway length is the amount of runway you have left to work with after allowing for clearance of any obstacle that would interfere with the use of the entire runway. In either case, the short-field technique should be used to take off or land safely.

Short-Field Takeoff

Assuming you are taking off from a short field, or a field with an obstruction, strive to fly your aircraft by airspeed and attitude control rather than letting your instincts take over. If you get caught in the trap of trying to clear an obstruction or take off before your aircraft is ready to fly, the results can be most unpleasurable—even deadly. If you try to force the aircraft into the air before it is ready to fly, it just might drop back onto the runway. This may in fact even lengthen the time it will take you to clear the obstruction. If this is allowed to happen, you may not make it at all.

A good habit to get into is to use every available inch of runway as you line up to practice short-field takeoffs. Any runway you leave behind you before you actually begin your takeoff roll may as well be in another state. It will be of no use to you since you didn't take advantage of its availability in the first place. Use it *all*.

Utilize the manufacturer's recommended flap setting if your aircraft is so equipped. Line up on the centerline and—using *all* of the available runway—smoothly but firmly add full power. Don't hold your brakes. Get going!

Studies have shown that unless you are in a turbine-powered aircraft, holding the brakes while running the engine up to maximum rpm before brake release does nothing to enhance your short-field

Fig. 5-19. Soft-field touchdown. Full stall, full flap, and full back elevator to help prevent any noseover tendency.

takeoff distance. It may, in fact, hinder your acceleration and thereby lengthen your takeoff roll. The reason for this is that since the prop is an airfoil, it is thereby governed by certain laws of physics. As you know, an airfoil creates uneven pressures—high pressure beneath and low pressure above. In the case of the prop, the lower pressure is created in front of the propeller, causing its effectiveness to be diminished since the prop is "biting into" the area of lower pressure. This causes loss of thrust, which in turn causes loss of acceleration and thereby increases your short-field takeoff roll. This is the way it was explained to me by an aeronautical engineer.

Smoothly apply full power and let your aircraft accelerate until you arrive at the best angle-of-climb airspeed (V_x). Keep your aircraft straight down the centerline and let it seek its own pitch attitude. That is, don't force your nose down while you are accelerating for it will likely give you a negative angle of attack and increase the distance needed to arrive at V_x. When you arrive at V_x, rotate and maintain that airspeed until you have safely cleared any obstruction (Fig. 5-20). After clearing the obstruction reduce the angle of attack and allow your aircraft to accelerate to its normal climb speed. Your flaps, if required, should be left in the takeoff position until you have safely cleared any obstruction. They may then be brought up slowly, watching for any sign of a tendency for the aircraft to sink.

While on the subject of short-field takeoff technique, I would like to bring up a difference of opinion between instructors, pilots in general, and the FAA. Some of the instructors you run into will tell you that to get better performance on a short-field takeoff you should rotate just a few knots before you arrive at V_x. Their thinking is that by the time you rotate, you will have accelerated to V_x and

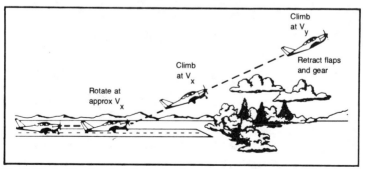

Fig. 5-20. Profile of a short-field takeoff. (courtesy FAA)

everything will work out better. They also claim it is almost impossible to rotate at, and maintain, V_x. The FAA's own handbook says they are wrong. I say they are wrong. Many aircraft flight manuals say they are wrong. In short, they are wrong. If it's beyond their capability to perform a short-field takeoff correctly, that's their problem. Precise pilots should rotate at, and maintain, V_x. It is the only way to obtain maximum performance from your aircraft. In most short-field takeoffs, the primary ingredient for success is maximum performance—both aircraft and pilot.

Short-Field Landing

Short-field landings should always be practiced assuming that a 50-foot obstacle exists on the approach end of the runway. The approach to a short-field landing should be made with power as needed and at an airspeed of no more than 1.3 V_{so} (1.3 times the power-off stall speed with your gear and flaps down). A competent pilot should be able to execute the approach as slowly as possible, consistent with safety.

Your traffic pattern will be pretty much normal until you are on final. On final approach you will find the key to establishing your short-field technique. This key involves obtaining a clear visual and mental picture of a straight line from your position on final, over your obstruction, to the point of intended touchdown. Once you have set up this mental picture, attain the desired airspeed and control your descent using coordinated power, flaps, and proper pitch attitude. If you do it correctly, your power will be slowly reduced until it reaches idle just as you are in the landing flare. The point I'm trying to make is that a short-field approach is a power approach. As you no longer need power, you slowly get rid of it. Naturally, if you see that you are going to be short, use additional power to re-establish your glide path. That is, if you are only a little below your glide path, the addition of a small amount of power and a slight pitch change should put you right back where you want to be. If you see that you are going to be *way* too low, the prudent thing to do is abandon your approach and go around and try it again.

The touchdown for a short-field landing should come at your minimum controllable airspeed, power at idle, and with little or no float. Retract your flaps as soon as possible after touchdown in order to place the aircraft's weight back onto the wheels; this will result in better braking action.

Aside from improper pitch and power control, there are two very common and potentially dangerous errors in the execution of the short-field approach and landing. One is a tendency to lower your nose after you have cleared the obstruction. The problem here is that the lowering of the nose will increase your airspeed, which results in the aircraft floating down the runway, eating up huge chunks of distance, rather than touching down short as it would have had you held your attitude constant all the way down to the flare (Fig. 5-21). As you might imagine, this could lead to an overshoot, which could spoil the whole maneuver—as well as your aircraft, your day, and possibly even your body.

The second error is reducing the power to idle as you cross over the obstruction. This procedure can be very dangerous; since you are approaching at a very low airspeed, the sudden loss of thrust can lead to an immediate stall. Not exactly what you had in mind, right? Oh, yes, it will definitely give you a short-field landing, but it just may be a little shorter than you had bargained for. It is because of this very error that the FAA some years back changed their minds on the correct procedure for a short-field landing. They were having a rather busy time going out and investigating short-field approach accidents that were caused by pilots reducing their power too early, stalling, and creating all kinds of messes a short distance down the runway. The thinking then changed to the constant-attitude/power-controlled approach. And it is indeed much, much safer.

Strong or gusty winds can cause the short-field approach to become a little treacherous. I believe you would be wise to carry a little extra power and airspeed in these conditions. In strong winds, the ground speed of your aircraft is slowed considerably so a bit

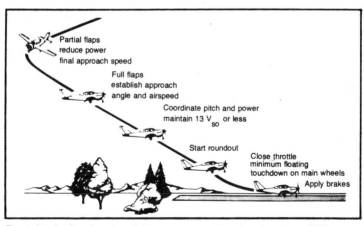

Fig. 5-21. Profile of a short-field approach and landing. (courtesy FAA)

more airspeed is needed to make up for it and thus add a greater margin for safety. Gusty winds are even more troublesome. Once again, the power and airspeed should be a little higher than normal. On your approach, if the wind you are riding suddenly dies, your aircraft is likely to sink rapidly and leave you with little or no time to recover—especially on short final, when you are very low to the ground. More than one pilot has fallen victim to this bit of treachery. Remember, there is a vast difference between a short-field landing and landing short of the field.

If you have trouble with normal short-field approaches, return to approaches at $1.3 \ V_{so}$ and then gradually work your way down to slower speeds. Don't try to force proficiency from yourself before you are ready to handle it. Short-field techniques require a high degree of reflex and feel for your aircraft. These are things that cannot be taught by the best instructor. They must be acquired by trial, practice, and time.

GO-AROUNDS

One of the most important things a truly precise pilot carries in his mind is the fact that not all approaches may be successfully completed. Maybe you have misjudged the wind and fouled up your approach. Perhaps you are too high or too low to comfortably complete your approach, or possibly someone has pulled out onto the runway in front of you. In any case, the prudent thing to do would be to go around and try it again. Many pilots feel a go-around is a sign of poor pilot technique, a lack of piloting skill, or just plain embarrassing. *Wrong*. A go-around, initiated when it is needed, shows that the pilot is thinking safety, has a good grasp of the situation, and would rather let the lesser pilots razz him than compromise his safe flight techniques.

Generally speaking, a go-around is merely a transition from your approach configuration through level flight and back to a normal climb attitude. A small dose of common sense, along with a little thought, should help you realize the ease and importance of this action. If you have blown your approach, the go-around may be executed as you continue your path straight down the runway. If someone has pulled onto the runway in front of you, it would be wise to move off to the side, thus allowing you to keep the other traffic in sight as you continue your go-around. Since you will most likely be in the left seat, this would mean moving off the runway to your right—just to the side of the runway, not into the next county. The main thing is to move out of the path of the other traffic and, at the same time, keep him in sight.

Let's say you're on short final with full flaps and your power near idle when you see the need to execute a go-around. Proceed with the following steps:

- [ ] First, add full power as you begin to transition through level flight to a normal climb attitude.
- [ ] Second, push off your carb heat in order to develop full power.
- [ ] Third, bring up your flaps to the manufacturer's recommended go-around setting. This will decrease your drag and allow for better acceleration.

After completing all three steps, make sure you are at least at V_x airspeed, holding your own—or better still, climbing. When you are positive that your airspeed, heading, and attitude are stable, retract your flaps the rest of the way, allow the airspeed to climb to V_y, and continue your normal climbout.

In the event the situation requires a side-step maneuver to avoid another aircraft, your go-around should be completed as above except that you will have to do it while executing a shallow turn away from the traffic. Unless the situation requires your immediate action, I believe you will find it safer to get your power up and your aircraft cleaned up before you attempt the turn. This way you will not get involved in a low-airspeed, low-power, flaps-down bank—which can prove to be a handful, even for a very experienced pilot.

There is one other problem that might necessitate a go-around—a good old-fashioned bounced landing. If you haven't done a few yet, hang around; you will. Most often the bounce is slight and you should be able to recover using a little power, lowering your nose back to level flight attitude and then flaring again. That's *most* of the time.

If you really bounce it by dropping it in from about 15 feet and spread out your spring-steel gear to the point that it groans, snaps back into position, and sends you about 39 feet back toward your approach altitude, you just might want to consider a go-around. Let's face it: You're already up there, so you might as well go ahead and go around. When this calamity befalls you, above all, *remain calm*. Then quickly add full power, lower your nose back to level flight attitude, and accelerate to your normal climb airspeed as you slowly retract your flaps to the manufacturer's recommended go-around setting. You will most likely experience a little sink as you bring the flaps up, but do not pull your nose up yet. Leave your pitch at about level flight attitude so you can accelerate quicker. Complete your go-around heading straight down the runway and climb out normally. Usually the next landing will be much better, if for no other reason than you will have probably gotten your own attention and will not want an instant replay of your previous arrival. I say *arrival* since it is quite obvious that whatever transpired on your last attempt, a landing it was not.

Before we leave takeoffs and landings altogether, I would like to offer an observation that I realize is debatable, but here it is anyway: Touch-and-go takeoffs and landings have no place in primary flight maneuvers. I firmly believe they are a total waste of the student's time, money, and learning process. I mean, how can you practice a short-field or soft-field takeoff if you never get below 35 knots? You can't. Further, the student is cheated out of one of the most important elements of learning to fly—learning to feel the change in control effectiveness as the airspeed increases and decreases. This is such an important point but one that I'm afraid too many flight instructors take much too lightly. Oh, sure, you can get in quite a few more takeoffs and landings using the touch-and-go method, but the *real* question is: How effective is the time put forth in shooting touch-and-goes? Not very, I believe. Changing conditions, changing winds, and changing speeds are what flying is all about. You just don't get the full benefit of these changing conditions if you shoot touch-and-go takeoffs and landings.

Many pilots refer to this process as shooting "bumps and circuits," "bounce and goes," and several other rather apt names that reflect the true amount of learning which takes place during such a practice session. Now really, wouldn't you rather execute a takeoff and a landing as opposed to a "bounce and go?" I would, and I hope that you have enough foresight to realize which one will give you the fullest benefit during your learning process. I also hope that you really want to be the best pilot you can possibly be. We already have enough people flying around who really don't care about proficiency. If you think I'm kidding, just read a few accident reports. You will find the vast majority are summed up as "pilot error." And pilot error is bred by, for the most part, neglect, disdain, and downright disregard of the formation of correct habit patterns during the learning process. For your own sake, learn it right.

Chapter 6

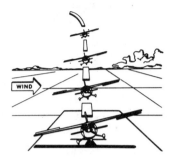

Emergency Procedures

Emergencies come in all shapes and sizes. They can range from a complete engine failure to fire, equipment failure, loss of radio communications, flat tires, and just about anything else you can think of. In fact, what may seem to be an emergency to one pilot may be nothing more than an inconvenience to another. It is impossible to cover every conceivable emergency that you may run into (Fig. 6-1). Every emergency, however, has one thing in common: They all require action. And if you have a *true* emergency, that action had better come quickly and accurately. It should be, in most cases, a conditioned response brought about by many hours of practice and forethought. It is one of the few places in aviation where a pilot should operate almost from rote, a conditioned response limited only by the pilot's experience and training.

Some emergencies are much more serious than others. Sometimes, as in an engine failure at high altitude, you will have plenty of time to get organized and proceed accordingly. Other times you will be called upon to make split-second decisions—and they had better be the correct ones or you just might ruin your whole day.

ENGINE FAILURE

Let's discuss the problem that usually pops into a pilot's mind first when you speak of an emergency—engine failure. This particular emergency may be very dangerous or no big deal, depending on where it occurs and your readiness, training, and reaction.

Fig. 6-1. Carefully checking the things that you may take for granted can often prevent big trouble later on.

Whether the power loss is total or only partial will also make a difference. If you experience a partial power loss, however don't become too relaxed since engines that lose some power have a rather nasty habit of rapidly losing the rest.

Generally speaking, there are three distinct actions that you should complete, quickly and in order, if you suffer a power loss:

☐ Set up a glide.
☐ Make a thorough cockpit check.
☐ Look for the best possible place to land.

Glide

Let's go through the three actions and determine why they should come one at a time, in this exact order. If you are anywhere other than on the ground (which is the best place to have an engine failure), what is the most important thing you have going for you? *Altitude*—altitude buys you time. It allows you time to think, act, call for help, or let someone else know that you are having problems. Altitude gives you time to prepare yourself and your aircraft for an emergency landing and time in which to pick the best possible spot to land. At most altitudes you will even have time to attempt a restart. Yes, altitude buys you precious time, so in order to make the best use of that time, don't allow your aircraft to descend in a cruise airspeed-type descent, which eats up huge chunks of altitude very rapidly; set up a glide using the manufacturer's recommended best glide speed and use that altitude for something more useful (Fig. 6-2). That's Number One.

Cockpit Check

Number Two is a thorough cockpit check. Notice I said *thorough*. Having set up your glide and assuming you are at a reasonably high altitude, you should have time to investigate and maybe find and correct the cause of your power loss. Perhaps you need carb heat to rid yourself of a small amount of ice, or maybe you merely need to switch to another fuel tank—one with some fuel in it.

You just might be surprised at the number of major accidents that have been caused by some very minor problems. Many of these problems can be overcome with a proper cockpit check.

When you make your cockpit check, go directly to the most likely sources of power loss such as the carb heat, fuel selector valve, mixture, mags, and primer. Do not go for them in some random pattern, though, which might cause you to overlook something very important. Do it in an orderly fashion. If time and altitude permits, use your written checklist. The chances are you will be in some degree of shock from the sudden power loss and your written

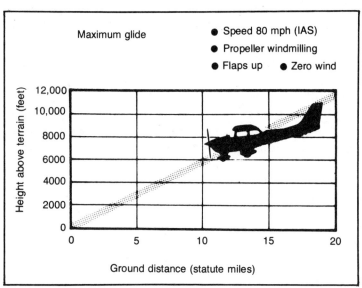

Fig. 6-2. It's a good idea to become very familiar with the best glide speed and glide ratio chart for your aircraft. (courtesy Cessna)

checklist will make it much more unlikely that you forget to check something that could prove to be very important.

If you don't have time, or if you can't find your written checklist, I have a method I teach for use in an emergency situation that is pretty complete and takes about three seconds. It is done mostly by rote and can be applied to most light aircraft.

For example, as you are setting up your glide, you are putting in some trim to help stabilize your airspeed at the best glide speed. Since your hand is already on the trim tab, it is an easy and short motion to drop your hand down and check the fuel selector. Then bring your hand up and start at the right side of the panel; check your mixture to be sure it is in the full-rich position. The rest of your planned motion proceeds to your left across the panel. Check your carb heat (which should be pulled on at the very beginning), the mags (which really should be checked one at a time), and the primer (which should be in and locked). That's it. You have covered the main points in very quick fashion and are ready to proceed to your next move.

I have found this method to be very useful in a lower-altitude emergency situation where you just don't have time to fumble for a written checklist. At the risk of repetition, I want to make one point perfectly clear: If you have the time and altitude, use your written checklist. It could save your life.

Turning into the Wind

Step Number Three is to turn into the wind, or crosswind, and locate the best possible site for you to put it down. Of course, this step should be taken only if you have not been successful in obtaining a restart. In this event, you will want to put your aircraft down as slowly as possible and with as much control as possible. The cardinal rule of emergency landings is, "If you know you are going to have to land, or crash, go in with as much control as possible." This is the only way you will have any control over your own destiny (Fig. 6-3). Remember, an aircraft that lands, or crashes, out of control is often fatal to the parties involved. So if you have no other alternative except to land, pick your spot and maintain as much control over your aircraft as you can. The chances for your survival will be greatly increased.

EMERGENCY LANDINGS

If you ever have the memorable experience of having to make an unscheduled landing in an emergency, how do you go about

Fig. 6-3. If you know you are going to have to put your aircraft down, go in with as much control as possible. (courtesy FAA)

selecting the most suitable landing site? I have a set of rules that I follow and try to impart to my students as to the order of places in which I would try to land in the event of a forced landing. The first—and most obvious—choice is an airport. They really are the best places to land, you know. I have heard of several pilots who became so overwhelmed by the heat of the moment that they actually landed in a field directly *beside* an airport—sort of embarrassing, and not too safe, either. My second choice is a road, vacant of traffic and void of power lines. The greatest deterrent to landing on a road is that unless you have some experience in dealing with such things, the power lines are often hard to detect until it could be too late to do anything about it. Also, there is the matter of judgment of the highway traffic. It is not nice to land on top of a group of old ladies on their way to church—spoils everyone's day. Besides, it is your responsibility to take every option open to you in order to prevent any injury to innocent people on the ground.

My third choice is a pasture, either hay or wheat, freshly cut or early in the season so it will be short, greatly reducing the chances of the aircraft nosing over after touchdown.

All the rest of the alternatives follow in a rather random order, as none is very conducive to a successful landing in an emergency (or any other time): a field of standing corn, beans, etc., and lakes, rivers, plowed ground, areas of trees, and rocky fields.

If you know that you are going to have to land in a field of any kind, you will be far better off to attempt your landing *with* the rows rather than *across* them (Fig. 6-4). You severely diminish your chances of remaining upright when you attempt a landing across rough ground. Anything that reduces your chances of remaining upright also increases your chances of bodily injury. Other than innocent people on the ground, the most important thing you need to salvage is yourself. The aircraft manufacturers are making aircraft every day. They're not making any more of you and me, you know.

I once saw the results of a practice emergency landing where the instructor had the poor judgment to allow the student to attempt a real landing in what they thought to be a suitable landing area. It turned out to be mud. No one was injured, though the aircraft was a little worse for the experience. I think this incident should convey at least two points: one, unless you are landing on an airport, don't ever really land out of a practice emergency approach. Sometimes the most urgent emergency comes *after* the landing. And two, not all landing areas are what they seem to be from the air. It takes time and experience to judge from altitude the makeup of a given landing area, and even then you may not always be correct in your decision. The point I'm trying to make is that aircraft are made to land on something that resembles a hard, smooth surface. For the most part, aircraft landing gear cannot withstand landing on rough, uneven surfaces.

POWER FAILURE ON TAKEOFF

If you suffer a power loss during the takeoff roll, reduce your power (if you have any left) to idle and abort the takeoff. Don't

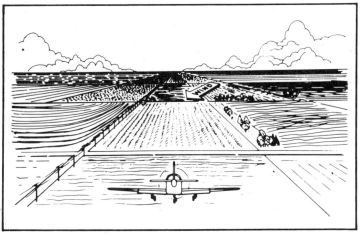

Fig. 6-4. If you ever have to land in a field, your chances of remaining upright are greatly improved if you land with the rows. (courtesy FAA)

attempt to struggle into the air with an aircraft that is not developing full power. It's suicidal.

If you suffer a power loss after liftoff, there will be several factors to take into consideration to determine the correct moves. These items include the degree of the power loss as well as your altitude at the time of the failure, runway remaining, and possible obstructions to your flight path. A general rule, recommended by the FAA and taught by most flight instructors, is if you are not at least 400 feet above the surface, continue on straight ahead, take whatever comes, and land as slowly as possible. Most pilots just cannot execute a 180-degree turn and return and land safely from anything less than 400 feet above the ground. Many have tried; few have made it. Most stall during the turn or simultaneously run out of airspeed, altitude, and ideas. The result is usually predictable and disastrous. If you have witnessed an aircraft attempting to return to its original runway from an unsafe altitude and catch a wing tip and cartwheel out of control, throwing pieces of metal and people in all directions—as I have—you would think several times about attempting that deadly 180-degree turn back to the runway. Your chances for survival will be greatly enhanced if you just continue on, straight ahead, and land your aircraft in a slow, controlled manner.

The problem with this type of low-level power failure is that the urge to turn around and attempt to return to the safety of the runway is almost overwhelming. Many experienced pilots have forgotten everything they ever learned in such an instance and tried to turn around. It is as if their brain is in a holding pattern. The results are usually very unhappy (Fig. 6-5).

Learning to avoid such an urge will take a great deal of practice and self-discipline. Take your aircraft up to a safe altitude and simulate a takeoff by slowing your aircraft down to your liftoff speed, then apply full power and initiate a climb. Decide what altitude you wish to use for the "ground." Continue your climb until you are exactly 400 feet above your "ground" altitude. Now pull your power to idle and, as rapidly as possible, execute a 180-degree turn. Did you go below your "ground" altitude? Chances are that you did. If you didn't, how close did you come to it? Remember, you were *ready* for this practice emergency. In the case of a real situation, you will have the element of surprise, and this will work against you. Try this exercise a few times and see what your optimum turnaround altitude is. I would then suggest that you add a couple of hundred feet to this altitude for safety. When you are near the ground things can tend to move a little quicker; you are far more

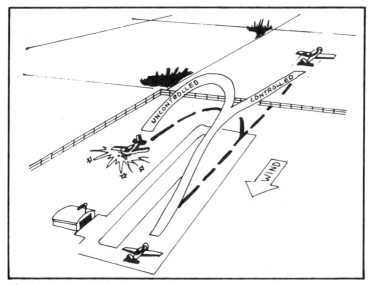

Fig. 6-5. If you experience an engine failure during climbout, the urge to attempt a return to the airport can be overpowering, and usually disastrous. (courtesy FAA)

likely to over-pull on your back pressure and induce an accelerated stall.

Before leaving the subject of the 180-degree turn, I'd like to point out that there are several variables that will affect your aircraft's turnaround time. Don't forget that your takeoff weight may not always be the same. The temperature and the density altitude also have a large effect since they are rarely the same on any two given days. The last variable is the wind. Although the wind will have no affect on your airspeed, it can give you a false sense of going faster than you really are, thus drawing you into a possible accelerated stall. The wind velocity could also be so great as to blow you right back over the runway you want so badly to land on. See? There are many things that enter into your decision. Can you take them all into consideration and still make the correct decision? In an emergency? At low altitude? My advice is: Go straight ahead; don't try to turn around. You may not live to regret it.

If you encounter an emergency at from 400 feet above the ground up to, say, 1000 feet—the area I call *the zone of decision*—you will still have to take into consideration the factors of runway availability, obstructions, safe optional landing areas, etc. I believe that this area is the most dangerous place to suffer a power loss. There are so many options open to you that making the correct decision is sometimes difficult. The decision really boils down to this: Where can you land with the greatest chance of doing so safely? Forget the whats, ifs, and maybes. Go directly to the spot which offers the best chance for your safe landing.

In this zone of decision you should have time to set up a glide, make your cockpit check, and (if you cannot obtain a restart) pick the most suitable place to put your aircraft down safely. But you will have to practice your emergency procedures until they become automatic reflex actions. Emergency procedures should be almost mechanical. They have to be. Sometimes you just don't have time to get out the book and look up the solution to your problem.

I have had the occasion to make several emergency landings during my career in aviation, but fortunately most were of the precautionary type. One, I'm sorry to say, was not. On a hot summer day several years ago, two other instructors and I were going someplace in a Piper Apache. I don't remember where we were going because we never got there. We didn't even get close. For those of you not familiar with the Piper Apache, it is a four-place, twin-engine and rather low-powered aircraft. It was one of the first production twins that was affordable to pilots of near-average financial status. The Apache was a pretty good aircraft as long as both engines were running. It was not noted for its single-engine performance.

I was the lucky one elected to fly that particular day. With everything checked out and ready, we started our takeoff roll on our runway 27. The Apache accelerated rather slowly, mostly because we were at near gross weight and it was a very hot day. Our runways are 5200 feet long and I guess we had used about 1200 feet before we reached our rotation speed, safely above V_{mc} (velocity of minimum control), rotated, and were off.

At a height of about 30 feet above the runway, the right engine quit as surely as if it had never been there to begin with. I mean it didn't sputter, cough, or anything else; it just quit. Before I could react, the nose had swung about 20 degrees to the right of our intended heading and we were heading for the boonies—and *not* climbing. I immediately chopped the power to both engines, swung the Apache back to the runway, hit full flaps, landed, put the flaps back up for better braking, and stood on the brakes for all I was worth. We stopped with a little runway to spare. (I'm not going to lie to you and say we stopped with only an inch of runway left. We had two). Had we been on a shorter runway, we would have been commited to fly on and try to nurse the Apache up to enough altitude to circle around and return for a landing. But luckily we had started with a full mile of hard-surfaced runway to work with, so I made the decision to abort the takeoff and land because I thought it would be the safest thing to do for all concerned. And believe me, we all were concerned for a few moments.

Now, I didn't have all day to make my decision, nor did I bother to take a poll of those on board and let the majority rule. The decision was mine, good or bad. I had only to hope I was doing the correct thing. The point I'm trying to get across is that the decision was *reflex*—reflex that came from some very good dual instruction I had had in multi-engine emergency techniques and many hours of practice and forethought. The result was no damage to the aircraft or its occupants, although there was some talk of cleaning some seats after it was all over and done with.

Our problem was that a faulty fuel selector valve for the right engine showed to be in the "Right Main" position and turned out to be, in reality, off. If this teaches you anything, it might be that not all things are as they appear. You should be ready for the unexpected at all times.

This example brings to mind a point that I try to teach all of my students and try to remember myself. I call it the "What would I do if?" problem. When you are flying along, taking off or landing or whatever, look around and ask yourself, "What would I do if?" Try it. It's great fun and may make you aware of some things that you have never dreamed. Often I find myself at home sitting in a chair, thinking of a new situation and asking myself, "What would I do if?" It's almost as good as some dual—maybe better.

If you ever experience an emergency at an altitude above 1000 feet, follow the three rules we previously talked about. At these altitudes, you should have time to use your emergency checklist and be certain you have checked every possible emergency procedure before making the decision to land. This is especially true if you happen to be over hostile terrain (Fig. 6-6). You will want to do everything in your power to initiate a restart. Above all, take your time and try not to panic. Panic has caused some very routine emergencies to terminate with some very severe consequences.

Most good flight instructors know that a student who reacts in a poor or erratic manner during the simulation of emergency landings will most likely have a real problem if the emergency ever becomes a reality. All of us have our heart rate quicken when confronted by a threatening circumstance, and this is normal. Actually, this quickening of the heart rate and the increased flow of adrenalin is our

Fig. 6-6. What would you do, in this situation, if you had to make an emergency landing? (courtesy Cessna)

body's way of gearing us up to meet the challenge of the threatening situation. The problem is that some pilots react in a calm, efficient manner while others seem to use the extra blood and adrenalin to do *something*, whether it be right or wrong. They panic. All their emotions are so caught up in the survival instinct that they forget everything they have ever been taught, lose their thought process, and often wind up acting incorrectly. The results are often fatal.

A pilot should be able to react within the scope of his training and experience in a calm, efficient manner when he is faced with some sort of emergency. This calm, efficient action is the mark of a true professional. He doesn't let the emergency handle him; he handles the emergency. And you don't have to be a high-time pilot to be a professional. Professionalism is more an inward attitude.

There are many other types of emergencies that you may encounter during your aviation career. Most of you, however, will not ever come into contact with an emergency of any sort because flying is safe, and it's becoming safer everyday. Pilots are being better trained and aircraft and their powerplants are becoming more and more reliable. Although there are more pilots flying more aircraft now than ever before, the percentage of accidents versus hours flown is declining.

ACCURACY LANDINGS

I bet you thought I was going to leave these out, didn't you? I have included them here, in the emergency chapter, because their main purpose is for you to be able to land your aircraft on a given spot anytime the need should arise.

Accuracy landings are a very important part of every pilot's training. The ability to land an aircraft on a desired spot, with or without power, is a very conforting feeling. Although accuracy landings are surely fun to practice and are required on Private Pilot and Commercial Pilot checkrides, they have a much more serious purpose. They are absolutely invaluable in an actual emergency situation. If you practice this maneuver until you become adept at landing on your desired spot, it will take much of the seriousness out of many types of emergency landings.

The most common way to practice accuracy landings is to pick a spot on the runway and then attempt to land on, or within two hundred feet beyond, that spot (Fig. 6-7). Any landing made short of your spot must be considered a failure. You see, in an actual emergency, if you fail to make your point of intended landing, even by a few feet, the chances of your striking a fence or some other obstruction is greatly increased. For this reason, I never have my students practice accuracy landings using the end of the runway as their aiming point, as this leaves you absolutely no margin for error should you come up a few feet short. I tell them to use a runway centerline stripe at least a couple of hundred yards down the run-

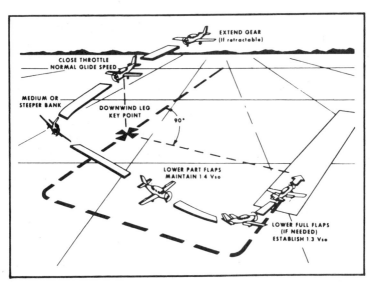

Fig. 6-7. Accuracy landing practice should become an important part of your training, now and always. (courtesy FAA)

way. This way you leave yourself a margin for small errors, which most of us mortals are inclined to make.

If you practice on a sod field, you may use anything that shows up well from the air. This could be a spot that has a different shade to it, or perhaps a slight rise or dip on the runway. The important thing is for you to pick a spot that you will be able to see all the way throughout your approach.

To begin your practice of accuracy landings, enter downwind at your normal pattern altitude and pick a prominent spot on the runway to use as your touchdown point. When your aircraft reaches a point adjacent to the spot, reduce your power to idle and initiate a power-off approach. Your pattern should be rectangular and as normal as possible. The use of flaps, slips or slight S-turning is fine as long as you don't get too carried away and start using dangerous maneuvers to help you arrive at your spot.

I find it best to turn onto final a little high, if possible, because you can always lose altitude by using the methods just mentioned. Be careful though, that you don't stay too high and wind up with the problem of an overshoot. Overshooting your spot in a real emergency can cause you just as much trouble as coming in short. Remember, this is an emergency procedure. In a real-life situation you will most likely have but one chance, and it had better be right. Taking your approach to the other extreme, if you are too low, there is no way on Earth you will get your aircraft onto the runway without any power.

Aim a *little* short of your spot to allow for your float during the flare. If you aim directly at your point, your float will carry you beyond your point of intended landing. The method I teach my students is the old moving spot technique. As you turn onto final, watch the spot of intended landing. If the spot appears to be moving towards you, you are too high. If, on the other hand, the spot appears to be moving away from you, you are too low. Of course, if you are way too high or low, you may not make the runway at all, or overshoot in the case of the former. It has to be within reason and it also depends on some variables such as how far out you are on final, airspeed, flap setting, etc. (Fig. 6-8).

If you find yourself too high while shooting an accuracy landing, you have several options. You may choose to add some flap, slip, or S-turn slightly, or perhaps a combination of several of these might be in order. If you see that you are going to be too low, the list of options is somewhat shorter. The best thing to do is maintain your best glide speed and withhold any more flap until you see if you are

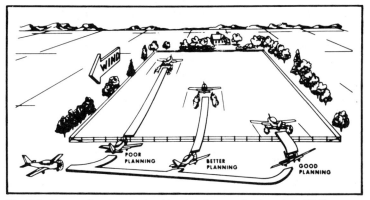

Fig. 6-8. Proper planning can lead to pleasing results. (courtesy FAA)

going to re-intercept your desired glide path. If this works, after you regain the glide path you desire, continue on with your approach and add flaps as needed to bring you to your desired spot.

There is one other option you have open if you see you are going to be too low. I will list it here with this word of caution: This method is for use only in a real-life emergency since it can do one of two things. It can get you where you want to be, sometimes, or it can get you into trouble if not properly executed. This maneuver can be very dangerous. When you realize that you will be too low to complete your approach to your preplanned spot, you might try trading the altitude you have left for airspeed. That is, dive your aircraft down to get it into ground effect and try to nurse it on in to the spot. It can work. You might be surprised at just how far along you can coax an aircraft in ground effect. You were going to be short anyway, so this method might get you onto safe ground—and with the added safety factor of landing as slowly as possible should you come up short.

Practice your accuracy landings with and without power and in full-flap and no-flap configurations. And practice them until you are confident you can land on a given spot from any altitude and power setting. Then continue to practice them often so you don't lose your touch. The knowledge that you can put your aircraft down on a given spot from any altitude at any time is of great comfort.

SPIRALS

Now that we have been over emergency procedures and accuracy landing, you might find it beneficial to learn one more time-proven method that you might use to get you down from a relatively high altitude while remaining over your point of intended landing. This method is the spiral.

Spirals are useful in your training to help you learn to remain oriented during prolonged descending turns. They are also of great help in increasing your ability to get your head out of the cockpit and still control your airspeed and bank. In the event of an actual emergency at altitude, the spiral is probably the best way to lose altitude and still remain close to your point of intended landing. A spiral is also useful when coming down through a hole in the clouds. This can help prevent you from the unpleasantness of having to try to explain illegal IFR flight to the Feds. I know of several pilots who have used this method to come down after becoming so engrossed in their practice that they failed to notice the broken layer they had at the start of the flight had become nearly overcast. I may have even done it once or twice.

Spirals are essentially a high-altitude maneuver to aid you in an emergency descent. Whether spiraling about a point to an emergency landing or coming down through a hole in the broken cloud layer, spirals usually indicate the need for a bit of prompt action on your part.

Spirals can be divided into two categories. The first is used in the instance I just mentioned. It is useful when coming down through a hole in the clouds or any other situation that calls for a rapid descent. Because this type of spiral does not include ground tracking, your main concerns are constant airspeed and bank while you descend to safety.

To begin your practice of this type of spiral, attain a fairly high altitude, clear the area around and below you, close your throttle to idle, set up a normal glide, and perform your cockpit check. Although this may not be an actual emergency situation, it is important that you maintain these habits. After clearing the area around and below, begin your spiral using about 50 degrees of bank. In this spiral, since ground track is not your major purpose, closely monitor the airspeed and bank control throughout the desired number of turns. Maintain, as closely as possible, the constant airspeed and bank through at least three turns. As a good safety practice, you probably should not spiral any lower than about 1500 feet above the ground. Continue to practice this spiral until you can perform at least three turns and keep your airspeed and bank constant. Remember, this spiral is for altitude loss; you need not worry about ground track.

The second type of spiral is the one in which you are concerned about your altitude loss as well as your ground track. This spiral is designed to help you remain over a given point on the ground. Incorporate the methods used in the previous spiral with a point about which to spiral. It then becomes more or less a turn-about-a-point in a gliding turn. Vary your bank as you would in a turn-about-a-point to maintain a constant distance from your pivotal point. Upon reaching pattern altitude, or slightly above, exit the spiral and enter a normal traffic pattern to get you to the point of intended landing (Fig. 6-9). The reason you want to try to use a normal traffic pattern is that the more familiar you can make the situation, the easier it will be for you to land on the predetermined point. Most pilots have a greater degree of difficulty landing out of a straight-in approach than from a normal traffic pattern. If you add the margin for human error (because an emergency situation often causes less-than-superior performance), I think you will begin to realize the need for establishing a normal traffic pattern.

I teach my students to fly to the downwind corner of the

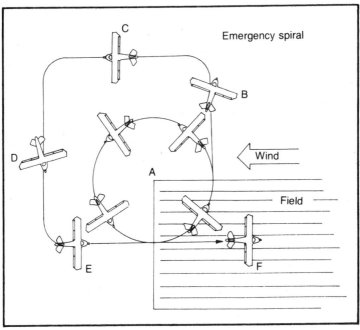

Fig. 6-9. Emergency spiral. (A) Spiral about the downwind corner on the downwind side of the field. (B) Break out a bit above normal pattern altitude. (C) Turn downwind. (D) Turn base. (E) Turn final a little high so you are sure you won't land short. (F) Land in field using a short- or soft-field technique as required. (courtesy FAA)

downwind side of the field on which they intend to land and then commence their spiral. This way they are in the best possible position to execute a near normal traffic pattern. For instance, if the field or runway on which they intend to land has a wind coming from the south, they would glide to the northeast corner of the field. They would then execute a spiral down to a position from which they could break out of the spiral on an easterly heading. From here they would merely have to turn left to be positioned on a downwind for the intended landing area. Now they are in a familiar situation from which they should have the best chance of landing successfully— and, I might add, safely.

Chapter 7

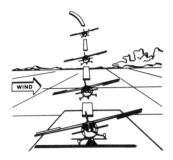

Basic Night Flying

Night flying is an important portion of the training of a precise pilot since night flying capability not only increases your aircraft utilization, but also provides you with the experience to handle night flight should you inadvertently fly into the darkness before you have had the chance to obtain some night dual. After you become proficient at night, you open a whole new world in your aviation spectrum.

The only real difference between day and night flight is that at night your vision is greatly restricted. This can cause a certain amount of fear and anxiety when you are just learning to fly at night. These fears can be overcome as you gain experience and insight into night flight and its peculiarities. As you gain confidence in your night flight ability, you may find that you actually prefer night flight since it is usually smoother and you will have less traffic to contend with.

NIGHT VISION

For some reason, many pilots and pilots-to-be are completely uninformed about night vision. Some know a little about the subject; others don't seem to care. The fact is that your vision is greatly affected by light and dark. The fact that you may be flying in either daylight or dark should make you want to know as much as possible about how your eyes work. If you learn how to use your eyes effectively, your night vision can be greatly improved. There are several reasons for training to use your eyes effectively for night flights.

One reason is that your mind and your eyes act as a team in order for you to see well. Also, the construction of your eyes is such that for you to see well at night, they must be used differently than they are in the daytime. Therefore, it is important that you understand how your eyes and your vision are affected by darkness.

Your eyes are full of innumerable light-sensitive nerves called *rods* and *cones*, which are located at the back of your eye, or *retina*. These nerves are connected to the optic nerve, which sends messages directly to your brain. The function of the cones is to detect color, details, and faraway objects. The rods' function is to give you peripheral vision, the ability to see out of the "corner of your eyes." The rods detect objects, particularly those that are moving, but give no detail or color, only shades of gray. Both your rods and your cones are used for vision during the daylight, but at night the visual process depends almost exclusively on the rods.

The fact that your rods are distributed in a band around the cones and do not lie directly in the center, behind the pupils of your eyes, makes "off center" viewing important during night flights. This means that your eyes see things best during the daylight when you look directly at them. At night, though, your eyes function best if you look slightly to the side of the object you are trying to see. Therefore, you can see more at night if you scan around the area you wish to see instead of trying to look directly at it (Fig. 7-1). This point is very important. I have often caught a glimpse of something at night, such as a rotating beacon at an airport, and then found myself staring at the spot I thought I would find it again when it reappeared. What I needed to do was look in the area *around* the spot instead of directly *at* it. In this manner I would pick up the object with my peripheral vision. Try it. Once you get used to the idea, your night vision will greatly improve.

The way your eyes adapt to darkness is another factor that is important to your night vision. You know that when you come out of the light into a dark area, such as a movie theater, it takes your eyes some time to adjust to the darkness. Just how long it takes may really surprise you. The cones, which you use for daylight vision, adjust to the dark after about 5 to 10 minutes. Quite a while, huh? Well, get ready for this: The rods, which you use almost exclusively for night vision, take about *30 minutes* to adjust to darkness after having been exposed to a brightly lit area. This means that for 30 minutes after you have exposed your eyes to a bright light, you will

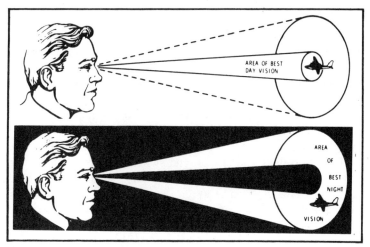

Fig. 7-1. Area of best night vision is in an area that surrounds the area of your best day vision. (courtesy FAA)

be operating your aircraft with much less than your full potential vision. Do you realize how far you can go in 30 minutes, how many possible situations you can encounter with less-than-full night vision capability? Think about this the next time you get bored during a night flight and decide to look into your flashlight while it's on.

The point is that you must learn to let your eyes adapt to the darkness and then do your best to keep them that way. After you have let your eyes become adapted to night vision, avoid exposing them to any bright light that could cause temporary night blindness.

Another possible side affect of temporary night blindness is illusion that take place during the time your eyes are recovering from a bright light. I know you have had the experience of looking at a bright light at night and then looking away and seeing spots and dots and all sorts of funny things. This can cause you big trouble. It doesn't matter whether you are a novice or experienced pilot, eyes are eyes and they react the same for all of us. These illusions can cause you to believe a town is an airport, or that clouds are the horizon. Recognizing that your brain and eyes can play tricks in this manner is your best protection for flying at night.

Good eyesight also depends on your physical condition. Fatigue, colds, medicine, vitamin deficiency, alcohol, and smoking can easily disrupt your vision, day or night. I have heard it said that smoking has an especially bad affect on night vision. Forewarned is forearmed. Keep these facts in mind and you will be off to a good start for your night flight learning process.

PILOT EQUIPMENT

Carefully consider the equipment that you should have readily available during the conduct of night flights. Much of this equipment won't differ greatly from that which you carry around most of the time anyway, but at night you will want to have it right where you can reach out and lay your hands on it quickly.

Probably the single most important piece of equipment to have at your side is a good, reliable flashlight—preferably one with a red lens that may be quickly switched to white. You can use the white while you preflight the aircraft and switch it over to red for use inside the cockpit. Some pilots I know even go so far as to carry *two* flashlights, one white and one red. A word of caution: A red light used at night to look at your aeronautical charts will cause some of the red features and lines to show up very poorly.

Other important items to have at hand include your charts, clipboard, map cases, pencils, extra flight plans, and all the common sense you have at your disposal. You should also have a reliable clock for either day or night operations.

No matter what items you need to have on board, the most important thing is for you to have everything organized so you won't be fumbling around in the dark trying to locate something. Use a checklist if you must to be sure you have everything and then be sure that everything has its place—and keep it there, for your own good.

AIRPLANE LIGHTING AND EQUIPMENT

Federal Aviation Regulations Part 91, specifies certain minimum equipment to have on board your aircraft for night operations. This equipment includes instruments, lights, an electrical energy source, and spare fuses. The list of equipment needed for day or night flights may be found in FAR 91.33.

Although not required by FAR 91, a wise pilot will not fly an aircraft that does not have an attitude indicator, heading indicator, and sensitive altimeter at night, especially when the pilot is new to flight operations. You see, at night there isn't always a definite horizon to go by and you will probably find yourself supplementing your visual flight by a cross-reference to these instruments.

Very important to your health and well-being—and also required by FAR Part 91—are your aircraft lights. You must have an anticollision light system; this includes an unmistakable flashing or rotating beacon and position lights. The beacon, as most pilots call it, can consist of either a red rotating beacon, usually positioned on top of the vertical fin, or a set of flashing white strobe lights. These strobe lights are usually positioned on either wing tip. Some aircraft have both the flashing strobes and a red rotating beacon. The main purpose of these lights, along with the position lights, is so you will be seen by other aircraft at night more readily.

The position lights are (just as their name implies) positioned exactly the same on all aircraft so you can tell the direction of flight of another aircraft just by the relative position of the lights as viewed from your cockpit. These lights are arranged at each wing tip and at the top of the tail of every aircraft that flies legally at night. The position light on the left wing tip is always red. The one on the right wing tip is always green. And the one on the tail is always white (Fig. 7-2).

If you are flying along at night and see a red light and a green light, this aircraft is heading in your general direction and you had better take notice since you might have to do a little maneuvering to avoid it. The old formula for remembering danger is "Red, Right, Returning." In other words, if you see a red position light and a green position light, the only direction this aircraft could be heading is right at you since you can only see both position lights if you are directly in front of an aircraft. If you see only a red position light, that aircraft would be passing from your right to your left in relation to where you are looking. If you see only a green light, that aircraft

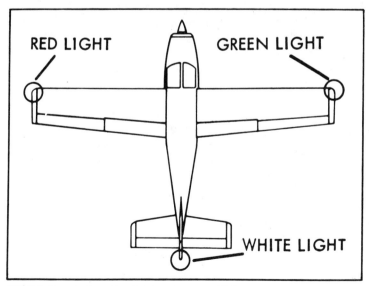

Fig. 7-2. Standard position lighting. (courtesy FAA)

would be passing from your left to your right. Last, if you only see a steady white light, that aircraft should be traveling away from you.

Next you will want a good landing light, which is useful for taxi, takeoff, and landing as well as providing a means by which other pilots may see you during flight. The FAA is encouraging all pilots to keep their landing lights on, day or night, while within a 10 mile radius of any airport as part of a "see-and-be-seen" safety program of collision avoidance. It's not a bad idea, really, especially when you are operating in conditions of reduced visibility. Personally, I would rather have my landing light on and replace it a little more often than get run over by a DC-9.

One more thought about aircraft lighting: Don't be led into complacency just because you have your lights on. And don't assume everyone else has theirs on, too. Light bulbs do burn out, you know. If you aren't watching very carefully, an aircraft light can blend in with the lights of a city or from stars and lead to a potentially dangerous situation. Increased awareness on your part will do more to forestall trouble than any other single factor I can think of.

AIRPORT AND NAVIGATION LIGHTING AIDS

You will also want to become familiar with the colors of lights used for runways, taxiways, obstructions, and other visual aids used to help you identify objects at night. Lighted airports located away from congested areas are readily indentifiable at night because their runway and taxiway lights stand out from the darkened surroundings. Airports located near or within cities, however, are often difficult to identify in the maze of lights. Therefore, it is important that you not only become knowledgeable about the airport's *exact* location, but that you also become very familiar with these airport's lighting pattern characteristics.

Airport lighting is designed and installed in a variety of colors and configurations, each with its own distinct purpose (Fig. 7-3). For instance, the rotating beacon that helps you to locate an airport will be seen as a series of light flashes that come at regular intervals. These flashes are either one or two different colors and are used to help you identify the various types of landing areas. For instance, an alternating white and green rotating beacon means you are looking at a lighted land airport. A white-only beacon means you are looking at an unlighted land airport. And if you see a beacon flashing a green and *two* whites, you are looking at a military airport.

Any obstructions or areas considered hazardous to aerial navigation are marked by beacons using red flashes. A steadily burning

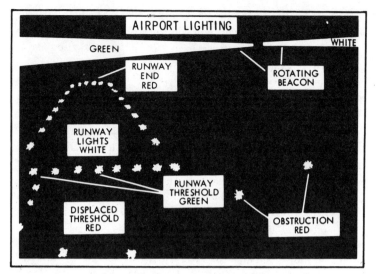

Fig. 7-3. Standard airport lighting. (courtesy FAA)

red light is used to mark obstructions on or near an airport, such as a water tower or tall building. Very high-intensity flashing white lights are now being used to make supporting structures of the tall power transmission lines that stretch across rivers, chasms, and valleys. These high-intensity flashing white lights are also sometimes used to mark tall structures such as chimneys and towers, such as you might find at a power plant.

The basic runway lighting system consists of runway-edge lights, one row on either side of the runway, which are white until you reach the last two thousand feet of the runway. They then can be a yellow color to indicate you are running out of runway. Of course, if you have a rather short runway, all of the runway lights will be white.

The runway threshold lights—the lights that identify the ends of the runway—are green on the approach end and red on the departure end. These lights are arranged across the runway directly at its end. Some airports have runway end identifier lights at the approach end of their runways. The abbreviation for these are REIL lights. These are flashing white strobe lights that I find very annoying on a VFR night. They tend to cause you to lose the night adaptation you have tried so hard to achieve just when you need it for landing.

The taxiway-edge lights are always blue. They outline the taxiway for you and are of great help in getting around an airport at night, especially if you happen to suffer the misfortune of losing your landing light. If you happen upon an airport that does not have these blue taxiway lights, use extreme caution in taxiing and go very slowly, using your landing light to your best advantage.

PREPARATION AND PREFLIGHT

Night flying requires that you have a complete realization of your abilities and limitations. Although any flight requires careful planning for maximum safety and efficiency, night flying demands more attention to the details of preflight and preparatory planning on your part (Fig. 7-4).

Your preparation for a night flight must include a thorough weather briefing—particularly the temperature/dewpoint spread, since the possibility of ground fog poses a greater danger than it would in the daylight. You should also be well aware of the wind direction and velocity because you will not be able to detect drift as readily during a night flight. A small error in navigation due to wind drift can lead you to assume that a town is the one you intended to be over when, in fact, you might be off a few miles. This, coupled with darkness, can get you lost very quickly.

Let me illustrate the subtle, innocent way in which the message of the preceding paragraph can nail you by relating a true night flight that happened to an author who shall remain nameless. I was returning to my home base from an airport about 200 miles away very late one night. I didn't bother to get a weather briefing (stupid) since it was an absolutely beautiful summer night. The sky was clear and the winds were light. Tired, but determined to go home, I headed out over a course I had flown many, many times. I was muttering to myself that the drone of the engine was making me

Fig. 7-4. Your preflight techniques prior to a night flight will require the same amount of attention you give to you and your aircraft during the daytime—and more.

sleepier than I already was when the lights of a familiar city appeared on the horizon—home. How good it was to be home.

I flew directly to the northeast corner of the city and began to prepare to land when it slowly dawned on me that my airport didn't seem to be there anymore. I flew over the area of the airport, looking to see if the lighting system had failed. It hadn't. I was at the wrong town. I was about 15 miles north of my actual homebase. You see, at night, the two cities are nearly identical and my navigation, or attention, must have suffered a bit and I mistook one city for the other. It can happen very easily, especially at night. But this is not the end of my tale.

I flew on toward my own airport, mad at myself for doing something as stupid as missing my own town, when I began to see a gray-white shadow forming on the ground all about me. Guess what? Ground fog—the warm summer night had lulled me into a trap. The air flowing over the cooling ground, combined with light winds, had cooled the air to its dewpoint. In fact, it was an almost textbook night for the formation of ground fog. I had been too stupid to get a weather briefing and now had almost outsmarted myself.

I flew on and arrived over my airport in just a few minutes. I knew it was there because I could see the rotating beacon sticking up through the fog. I could also see the tops of the trees and buildings. It seemed as if all of the objects coming up from the fog were tongues sticking out at me. The message they seemed to convey was, "All right, smart guy, what are you gonna do now?" I really wasn't sure.

I circled the airport a few times looking for a hole in the ground fog and trying to estimate its depth. I had enough fuel to go a bit farther; a quick call to the Flight Service people comfirmed that the fog was fairly widespread, but patchy. I decided the best solution was to orbit the airport for a while and hope a crack would appear that would allow me to land. A short time later a hole did appear over one of the runways and I landed quite uneventfully. But did I learn anything? You bet I did. I learned I was not my own best weather observer and nothing can take the place of a thorough preflight weather briefing and common sense. I knew better. I should not have let the beauty of the night lull me, a multi-thousand hour pilot, into such a stupid setup. You can bet it won't again, and I hope this little self-incrimination will help to save you from having to learn the hard way. Think it over.

If you are going to go on a night cross-country flight, plan it well and have all the pertinent charts marked well with prominently lighted checkpoints circled and noted. You will also want to note the position of airports along your flight path so you can deviate if need be. Check your radios, both communication and navigation, to be as sure as you can be that all are functioning properly.

Make a thorough preflight of your aircraft, checking all the lights as well as other normal items to be sure they are in working order. Any light not working should be replaced before any night flights are made—even locally.

In short, night flights require all the same preflight attention you give yourself and your aircraft during the daytime—and more. Be as sure as you can that both you and your aircraft are indeed ready for night flying. When you are, hop in and go have some fun.

STARTING, TAXI, AND RUNUP

When you get into the cockpit, buckle up, and prior to engine start, arrange all of your charts, etc., in the manner discussed previously. Make sure everything is in its place and that you are indeed ready to go. Don't hurry.

Follow your regular starting procedures with this added safety concern: Since it is night, the possibility of someone walking undetected near your aircraft is increased. For you and them to be aware of your imminent start, you should not only holler "Clear," but turn on your rotating beacon and flash your landing light a couple of times so they may readily see that something is about to happen. After you have done this, turn off all of the excess electrical equipment to help avoid draining your battery.

Next, turn on your master switch and your navigation lights. This is a standard warning to all concerned that you are about to start your aircraft. Also, you can check your navigation lights by looking for the glow they produce on the ground. After you start your engine and before you taxi out, turn on your landing or taxi light so you can look for any obstacle that might cause a problem. Most pilots use their taxi or landing lights sparingly while taxiing because the slow taxi speeds don't allow the heat to dissipate which can cause the light to burn out rather quickly. So unless you enjoy forking out bucks for landing lights, use them sparingly during taxi operations. Also, use common courtesy and try not to blind other pilots with your lights. There are few things that make me more unhappy than to get my night vision all adjusted and then have some joker swing around in my direction with about eight lights shining into my eyes. The thoughts that run through my mind at times like this may keep me out of Heaven.

At any rate, your night taxi procedures will be much the same as in the daylight except you may want to taxi a little more slowly and carefully (Fig. 7-5). If you are at an airport that has lines painted on the taxiways, for goodness sakes follow them. On a fairly bright night you may even be able to follow them without having to use your landing light. But be careful. Holes and ruts will not show up as well as you could conceivably put your nosewheel into a bad spot.

Your night runup should be as it is any other time with one exception. Your tendency to creep forward will not be as readily viewed at night. The solution is simple: Lock your brakes and apply your parking brake. This should alleviate any problems in this area.

TAKEOFF AND DEPARTURE

Although night flying is not a great deal different from daylight flying, it does demand more attention on your part. You will find the most impressive difference is the limited availability of outside visual references. Therefore, you have to depend more on your flight instruments to help you keep track of your attitude. You will find this especially true during your takeoff and departure climbout. Your cockpit lights should be adjusted to the lowest brightness that will allow you to see the instruments readily. This will also help eliminate the problem of your instrument lights reflecting on your windshield and windows, thus enhancing your night vision.

If you are operating from an uncontrolled airport, you will want to check for other traffic very carefully before taking the active runway. Make a 360-degree turn, in the same direction as the traffic

Fig. 7-5. "I told you a million times, turn on your taxi lights."

flows, to allow you to check both sky and ground for any possible conflicting traffic. Look very carefully since other traffic can blend in with the stars and be hard to detect.

After you are sure the final approach and runway are clear of traffic, pull past the hold lines and proceed directly to the runway centerline. If your airport has no centerline stripe, align your aircraft between the parallel runway lights as near to the center as you can manage. After you are lined up directly down the center of the runway, reset your directional gyro to correspond with the runway and double-check your fuel valve, mixture, carb heat, and engine instruments to be sure that all is ready.

Begin your takeoff as you would in the daylight. Advance the throttle slowly and smoothly, maintaining your alignment by use of the runway centerline or the runway edge lights. You will want to use your flight instruments a bit more than you do in the daytime since your speed will seem a little different in the darkness. As you accelerate, shift your eyes back and forth from your outside alignment to your instruments. Make sure you are remaining aligned with the centerline and that you are running all instruments in the green.

As your airspeed reaches normal liftoff speed, adjust your pitch to that which will establish a normal climb by referring to both outside visual references (such as lights) and to your attitude indicator. Do not force your aircraft off the ground. Let it fly off in liftoff attitude while you continue to cross-check your attitude indicator and outside visual references.

Now is the first time when night flying can get difficult. You will want to be sure that after you get airborne, you stay there. It is very important that you continue in a positive climb attitude and do not settle back onto the runway. Until you are used to night flying, this can be more difficult than it sounds. Be sure you have an indication of a positive rate of climb on your vertical speed indicator and that your airspeed is well above stall speed and accelerating. Also, check your altimeter to be sure it is indicating a gain in altitude. If all of these things check out, you're on your way.

Make any necessary adjustments in your pitch to establish a stable climb by using your airspeed and attitude indicators. At the same time, check to make sure your wings are level. It is not wise to attempt to turn at low altitude at night. Trim your aircraft to maintain a safe climb speed and, when everything is well in hand, turn off your landing light and continue your night climbout. I think you will find it exhilarating.

ORIENTATION AND NAVIGATION

As mentioned previously, you will want to be very aware of any possible traffic at night. Use the colors of other aircrafts' lights to help determine position and direction of flight.

At night it is difficult to see clouds, particularly on a very dark night or while flying under an overcast. If you are not really on the ball—and sometimes even if you are—you can fly smack into a cloud bank or fog layer in less time than it takes to say it. Usually, you will have some warning that you are about to enter an area of restricted visibility. Sometimes the lights on the ground take on a haze-like glow. This is a real clue that some form of obscuration is likely if you continue your flight in that direction. If the lights on the ground begin to fade and disappear, you are probably going to be in for a surprise very shortly. If this happens, all you can do is reverse your course and head elsewhere. You *do not* want to enter the clouds if you are flying VFR (Visual Flight Rules). Not only is it illegal, it is tantamount to suicide for a pilot without an instrument rating.

The maneuvers that you may practice safely at night are somewhat limited by your lack of a horizon. Straight-and-level, climbs, turns, and glides are among the first you should practice since you want to become familiar with your night senses. These naturally lead you into traffic pattern and landing work. Don't try anything silly. I have heard a pilot or two brag of doing night aerobatics. Even I, who have been accused of doing some pretty dumb things in an aircraft, have never dreamed of doing anything *that* stupid. I believe you'll find night flying quite exciting enough without tempting your luck.

If you go cross-country at night, remember your checkpoints will be fewer and use the methods discussed earlier. Use the light patterns on the surface that correspond with the details on your Sectional and watch carefully for any sign that you may be mistaking one city for another.

At night you can run into situations where the stars in the sky and the lights from the ground can seem to run together. This will leave you with no clear horizon and you will have to rely more heavily on your flight instruments. It will usually happen in sparsely populated areas away from large cities. If this does occur, you will also want to watch for any signs of vertigo.

Vertigo is a spatial disorientation in which you believe you are in an attitude different from the one your flight instruments are showing. If this happens, stay on your instruments and *believe* them. If you do, the vertigo will quickly pass. If, on the other hand, you believe your own bodily senses, you can be in for real trouble—even death. *Believe your instruments.*

One other problem that you may encounter at night is the altitude illusion. In this situation, lighted runways, buildings, or other objects that give off light may be seen very differently from one altitude than from another. For instance, at 2000 feet a group of lights or an object may be seen individually, but at 5000 feet or higher the objects can appear to be one solid light. These illusions can become quite acute as your altitude changes and if not overcome could present problems with respect to your approach and landing at lighted runways. What you need to do is to change your visual perspective as your altitude changes. Watch very carefully for any signs of ground lights showing you a different look. As you descend, a light that may have appeared as one large light may start to take on the look of several. Keep watching and when you get down low enough, try to discern what exactly it is you are seeing. Only by careful observation will you be able to refute the illusions your eyes see from altitude at night.

APPROACHES AND LANDINGS

When you arrive at an airport to enter the traffic pattern and land, it is important that you identify the runway lights and other airport lighting as soon as possible. If you are flying into an unfamiliar airport, you may have a problem finding the airport in the maze of lights that so often surrounds an airport near a city. The thing to do, then, is locate the airport's rotating beacon and sort of home in on it until you can begin to differentiate the runways from the maze.

Once you have the active runway in sight, carefully maneuver to your downwind and keep the runway lights in sight throughout your approach. This will give you a reference, a place to refer to in order to fly an appropriate traffic pattern. At night, distances can be deceptive due to the limited lighting conditions, lack of references on the ground, and your inability to compare the sizes and locations of ground objects. This same problem will show up in your estimation of altitude and speed. Once again, you will have to depend more on your flight instruments, particularly your altimeter and airspeed indicator.

Most inexperienced night pilots have a tendency to make approaches and landings at night with excessive airspeed. Many also approach at a much flatter angle than they should. Try to make your approach and landing the same as they are in the daytime. You might even want your approach to be a little steeper at night, especially at an airport with which you are unfamiliar since you are not sure as to obstacles and their placement. At any rate, a low, shallow approach at night is just asking for big trouble. Constantly check your altimeter and vertical speed indicator against your aircraft's position on base leg and final approach. In this way you can check your visual cues against your instruments and correct any errors before they become too prohibitive.

After you turn onto final approach, align your aircraft directly between the rows of runway lights and make any necessary corrections for wind drift. Coordinate your power and pitch for a positive approach, fully under your control and enabling you to make changes as necessary in your airspeed and approach angle. In other words, do whatever you have to do to keep your aircraft where you want it and at the speed you want it.

If you don't already have your landing light on for safety, turn it on about halfway down final. With all due respect to the FAA's "Operation Lights On," there are some nights when you just won't want your landing light on until you are very close in on final approach. These are the nights when your visibility is restricted by fog, haze, or smoke. Under these conditions your landing light can form a reflection that will adversely affect your night vision just when you need it most.

Make your roundout and landing in the same manner as you would in the daylight. Your judgment of height, speed, and sink rate will be impaired by the lack of visual reference points in the landing area. This often leads inexperienced night pilots to tend to round out too high. I believe this is because they are afraid of running into the ground. To help you determine the proper roundout point, maintain a constant approach descent until your landing light reflects off the runway and the runway's seams and tire marks can be plainly seen. At this point your roundout for touchdown should be started smoothly and your throttle gradually reduced to idle as your aircraft is touching down.

Another method of judging when to begin your roundout is to watch the runway lights. As you approach, they seem to be spaced widely apart. As you come down final they seem to begin to get closer and closer together. When they are almost in a line, you are getting very close to roundout time. The single most outstanding drawback to this method is that it requires a good deal of practice in order to get your timing down pat. I strongly advise you get some dual if you intend to try this method of judging your roundout starting point. While it works very well, if not properly executed it can get you into trouble because of the judgment involved.

If you get into a situation where you have to land without the aid of your landing light, some pilots utilize a method whereby they roundout when the runway lights at the far end of the runway appear to be higher than their aircraft. I don't like this method. I feel you are better off to use the runway-edge lights and sort of slow-fly your aircraft onto the surface. I offer it here only for your information since I feel this use of the far-end runway lights can easily make you misjudge your altitude and drive your aircraft into the ground.

If, on the other hand, your landing light is working but the runway lights are either nonexistent or out of service, your best bet is to first fly down the runway using your landing light to clear the runway. (By that I mean make sure you don't find any cattle wandering around grazing or other obstacles to interfere with a safe landing.) Then approach in a constant slow flight descent until your landing light picks up your area of intended landing, and then proceed carefully on to land. By the way, the clearing of your intended landing site is not a bad idea anytime, especially at an airport where there doesn't seem to be much activity.

NIGHT EMERGENCIES

The night emergency is perhaps the most dreaded aspect of nightflight for many pilots. You and I both know that the odds of your engine quitting are no more in the dark than they are in the daytime. But the results of that failure can be much more hazardous at night.

If your engine fails at night, your first step is the same as it is in the daytime: Set up a glide. Keep positive control of your aircraft, and try not to panic. After you set up a glide, altitude permitting, perform a cockpit check and attempt to restart the engine. And don't leave anything out. Check your fuel selector, mixture, mags, and so on until you are sure you will not be able to restart the engine. Don't dilly-dally around, even if you have thousands of feet of altitude. Find out whether or not the thing is going to run again.

Assuming a negative restart, you will want to turn toward an airport and away from congested areas, if possible. If you are not near an airport, at least get away from congested areas so the lights won't affect your night vision and for the safety of innocent people. Now orient yourself as to where the wind is coming from. This will be the direction you will want to land. If the night is so dark that you can't make out any terrain, at least you will be landing into the wind, which will give you the slowest possible ground speed at touchdown.

When you are low enough for your landing light to do you some good, turn it on and hope you see a suitable landing area. If not, your best bet is probably to remain heading into the wind and take whatever comes as slowly as you possibly can. Just before touchdown, you might be wise, depending on the terrain, to turn off your master switch in order to help prevent a fire should you not have a landing but an arrival. Above all, don't let your aircraft get out of control. Fly it in, don't merely go along for the ride. This way you have some control over your destiny. Remember, if you turn on your landing light and don't like what you see, turn it off. (Just kidding.)

Chapter 8

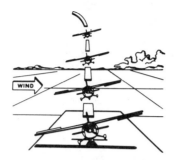

Basic Aerobatics

If you really want to sharpen your flying skills and become as precise a pilot as you possibly can, I can think of no better way to upgrade your coordination than to learn basic aerobatics. Aerobatics opens a whole new world in aviation—a world that will take you to higher dimensions of coordination and build your self-confidence to a point where you will really feel you are the master of your aircraft. Aerobatics will help you in every form of flying because it instills in you the confidence that only comes in knowing that the aircraft is merely an extension of your will. You know that when you move a control in a certain way, the aircraft will respond accordingly. This will carry over into all forms of flying. You will have better coordination. Your feel for the aircraft will be magnified. Your timing will become second nature and you will enjoy flying more. These are the positive rewards of learning basic aerobatics. In addition, aerobatics are fun!

Let's set some guidelines for safety. Although aerobatics can be self-taught, you would be wise to find a good instructor and get some dual before you venture out on your own. This way you can learn from someone who is experienced just what you should expect, what the common errors are, and, at the same time, have a capable pilot there to save your can when you mess up—and you *will*. As you might imagine, I have had more violent mistakes made by students during the course of dual in aerobatics than in all other forms of instruction I have ever given. I could devote an entire

Fig. 8-1. Bellanca Decathlon—a fine, modern aerobatic trainer.

chapter to stories about the fun I have had saving students from themselves during aerobatic dual. Some are funny and some are just plain stupid. Get some dual.

Second, don't ever try aerobatics in your friendly Cessna 152 or your Piper Cherokee. Use only an aircraft certified in the aerobatic category (Figs. 8-1, 8-2). To do otherwise is not only foolish, it can be—and often is—fatal. I have lost several friends who have been foolhearty enough to attempt aerobatics in aircraft not certified for aerobatics. A couple of these people were excellent pilots; they just used poor judgment, which proved fatal. Now don't get me wrong; aerobatics correctly done are not inherently dangerous—quite the opposite. The danger lies in attempting them in an uncertified aircraft or without proper dual in the aerobatic techniques.

Fig. 8-2. Boeing's Stearman is still used for aerobatics, but is rather clumsy by today's standards.

The FARs state that no one shall do aerobatics below 1500 feet above the ground. For practice, I would double this figure to give you more time to recover from your errors. In fact, you may wish to triple the 1500-foot minimum altitude so you will have plenty of room to explore, make your mistakes, and learn the precision involved in basic aerobatic flight.

In earlier chapters of this book we discussed the chandelle and lazy-8. These are limited aerobatic maneuvers and are very good for firming up your coordination and habit patterns so you may extend them into aerobatic flight. Let's continue on with an introduction to the basics of aerobatics.

WINGOVERS

The wingover is an excellent maneuver to introduce students to basic aerobatics. After mastering the lazy-8, the wingover should not pose too much of a problem. The wingover is nothing more than an exaggerated lazy-8. Your bank progression in the lazy-8 went from 0 degrees up to 30 degrees and back to 0 degrees. In the wingover you will at least double these banks from 0 degrees to 60 degrees and back to 0 degrees.

The wingover is started much the same as the lazy-8, but you will want to speed up the maneuver and your gain and loss of altitude will be greater. In the beginning, bring in your pitch a bit faster and follow with your bank. Then, when you arrive at approximately the 45-degree point, really crank in the bank, bringing it up to the maximum; the loss of vertical lift will allow your nose to fly back down through the horizon. At this time, reverse your bank and slowly reapply your back pressure to help bring the aircraft back to its original altitude, wings level and on a reciprocal of your entry heading. Your airspeed should also return to the entry speed.

As you learn to orient yourself in the wingover, you will be able to take it to extreme banks and still maintain positive control over the aircraft. The key is to keep the maneuver solid. By this I mean a positive G-load should be maintained at all times. If you begin to feel pressure on your shoulder harness, you are pulling less than one G and the chances are good that you are releasing too much back pressure at the 90-degree point. The aircraft should be *flown* through the maneuver, not followed—and this hold true for all maneuvers, aerobatic or not. I mean, after all, we are in search of precise piloting, are we not? Precision pilots do not follow their aircraft around the sky, they fly them.

Even in your practice of rather shallow wingovers, I suggest that you do not continue their practice for extended periods of time. Although they are great fun, they can cause even an old pro to become nauseated if done too long. And due to the large changes in altitude and heading, a wingover can get out of hand in a hurry, believe me. If one does get away, it is usually in the second half—the part where you are going downhill with cruise power and trying to recover from your steep bank. I have seen this happen many times. The pilot becomes disoriented and winds up heading downhill, airspeed increasing, in a very steep bank—and just sits there. The solution is to reduce your power to idle, quickly, then level your wings as you apply back pressure to regain level flight attitude.

The following are some words I hope you will never forget. If you ever get into trouble during aerobatics, whether you are dual or solo, your first priority is to *regain control over the aircraft*. Most problems come while you are either in a very steep bank (usually going down), or while inverted. Usually your first move will be to reduce your power to slow your descent. You then regain wings-level flight by either rolling upright or removing your bank. Then, and only then, increase your back pressure to return to level flight attitude. Putting it another way, get your aircraft rightside-up before you attempt to make any other recovery maneuvers. Most aircraft will gain airspeed at an incredible rate while diving inverted. The temptation is usually to pull back on the stick and split-S out of it. While this can work, you run the risk of pulling enough Gs to pull the fillings out of your upper teeth or snap your wings off. Slow it down. Get it rightside-up. Gently return to level flight.

SPINS

Spins, or the thought of them, do one of two things to a new pilot: They either evoke a surge of anticipation and excitement or they bring on a bad case of the shudders. It seems many people have an almost deadly fear of spins. I think much of this is brought about by too many "hangar flying" stories. I have heard so many of these stories during my time that tell of "spinning out" of a stall or some other maneuver. You want to know the truth? In this day of modern aircraft design, you have to work very hard to make your aircraft spin. Your Cessna 152 or Piper Cherokee, for example, are almost spinproof. They *will* spin, but not for long, and to get them into a spin is more trouble than it's worth, so when I here someone say they had an accidental spin out of some maneuver, my reply is usually to ask them if they ever did an accidental lazy-8. The chances are about the same.

I think part of the problem is the FAA. They label almost all aircraft accidents that occur below 5000 feet as "stall/spin" accidents. I believe (and this is only an opinion) that a more proper name would be "stalled/failed to recover." Oh, yes, if you stall an aircraft and let it go, a wing will drop for a time and you might even get as far as a 50 or 60-degree bank. But spin? No way—not in the true sense of the word.

A spin should be described as an aggravated stall that results in what is termed *autorotation* wherein the aircraft follows a corkscrew path in a downward direction (Fig. 8-3). The wings are producing some lift and the aircraft is forced down by gravity, yawing in a spiral path. The key is that the aircraft must be stalled in order to spin—and then, in our modern, stable aircraft, you have to work at it to remain in the spin.

Now, whichever side you wish to take makes little difference. The main thrust of all this is that if you learn to recognize the ingredients of a spin and then how to recover should you inadvertently spin anyway, you should be well-prepared for any and all possibilities. So let's learn how to properly enter and recover your aircraft from a spin.

The first thing you'll need in order to practice spins is altitude, and plenty of it. I suggest at least 4000 feet above the surface. You will then want to clear the area around and under your aircraft—and clear it well, because in a spin you will be plunging earthward, virtually out of control as far as maneuvering goes. Then line your aircraft up over a road. You will use the road to help you orient yourself during the spin as you may count the revolutions, or fractions thereof.

I usually have my students start by doing a one-turn spin so they can get the feel of the entry and recovery before they go for more revolutions.

Okay, you're lined up over a road, area cleared, and ready to spin. Smoothly reduce your power to idle as you bring the nose up to about 25 degrees above the horizon and keep it there as you would in a normal power-off stall. Then, just prior to a full stall, bring the stick full back into your stomach and keep it there. With full back stick and neutral aileron, stall your aircraft, and just as it stalls, add full rudder pressure in the direction you wish to spin. If you have everything in its place—aircraft stalled, full back stick, ailerons neutral and full rudder pressure—your nose will break off and roll in

Fig. 8-3. A two-turn spin. (courtesy FAA)

the direction of the applied rudder. You are in a spin. To maintain the spin, you must hold everything as is. That is, if you allow the stick to go forward, or reduce your rudder pressure, you will slide out of the spin and enter a very tight spiral. The only way you will notice this is by your airspeed indicator. In a spin, it stays at or near stall speed. Any increase in your airspeed is a sure sign you have slipped out of the spin, even though it may appear otherwise.

To recover from your one-turn spin, begin at approximately the three-quarter point of the revolution. Apply full opposite rudder (from the direction you are spinning) to stop the rotation. When the rotation ceases, ease forward on the stick to break the stall. Neutralize the rudder and your aircraft should fly itself out of the spin as you begin to apply back pressure slowly to return to level flight. When you reach level flight, advance the throttle back to your cruise setting. That's it—a spin entry, one turn, and a spin recovery. Nothing like the big, bad maneuver you have been told so much about, is it? Once again, knowledge is the key to precision and safety.

The most common error during recovery from a spin is the misuse of elevator. Once you have stopped the rotation with rudder, you may have trouble judging how much to allow the stick to come forward. If you don't allow it to come forward enough, you can inadvertently get a secondary stall. If you apply too *much* forward pressure, you will build up excessive airspeed and lose quite a bit of altitude. So allow your back pressure to go forward enough to feel as if you are flying instead of falling, and then smoothly reapply back pressure to bring you back to level flight attitude.

Remember, in order to enter a spin you must first stall the aircraft; to recover from a spin you must get out of the stall.

LOOPS

The loop was one of the first aerobatic maneuvers ever invented. It was used back in World War I to avoid other pilots while dogfighting over Europe. At first glance the loop looks to be a very simple maneuver, and it is. But making a loop really round takes a bit more technique than it would seem at first.

The loop, as you probably know, is merely a pitch maneuver that starts and ends at the same heading, altitude, and airspeed. But to make it come out right, you have to do a little more than just pull back. The loop may also come in various sizes, depending on how much initial G-load you want to pull. You see, the loop's size is predicated on the amount of back pressure you begin with. You may pull a low amount of back pressure and your loop will be rather large. Conversely, if your initial entry is accelerated, you will have a very tight circle. I once forgot to tell a student approximately how much back pressure to pull going into a loop and wound up with one that we could have done inside a hangar. Talk about G-loads! Live and learn, I guess.

Once you have visualized a loop, the next thing to learn, as in all aerobatic maneuvers, is where to look. Upon entry into a loop you will want to look forward over your nose until the horizon disappears. When this happens, shift your vision out to the wing tip so you can observe it and the horizon. Once you become inverted, again shift your vision back out the front windshield and pick up the horizon at this point. It sounds like the horizon is the key to aerobatics, doesn't it? It is. Without proper reference to the horizon, any aerobatic maneuver will suffer a great deal.

To initiate your loop, first clear the area around, below, and above your planned flight path. It is a good idea to practice your first few loops over a road. This way you can retain your alignment better over the ground because you will have the road to guide your path. Once you have selected a good area to practice loops, decide on an entry altitude and then climb above that altitude a few hundred feet so you can dive your aircraft to that altitude and proceed with your loop. The reason for this is that there are very few aircraft that will loop out of a normal cruise airspeed.

Area cleared, lined up over a road and a few hundred feet above your intended entry altitude, begin a shallow dive to pick up the necessary airspeed for your loop. Use the manufacturer's recommended entry speed. (If for some reason you don't know what speed is recommended, about 25 percent above normal cruise airspeed should get the job done.) If you are in an aircraft with a fixed-pitch propeller, take care not to exceed your tach redline. If you have a constant-speed prop, set your rpm and manifold pressure for normal climb setting and forget it (for now).

As you arrive at your entry airspeed and altitude, apply your back pressure smoothly; if you are in a fixed-pitch aircraft, also smoothly increase your power to it's maximum. As the aircraft continues upward during the first half of the loop, it will tend to lose airspeed and your elevator will begin to lose some of its effectiveness. This will necessitate ever-increasing back pressure to make up for this loss of control effectiveness and to aid in making the loop symmetrical (Fig. 8-4).

When you arrive at a point about 15 to 20 degrees before

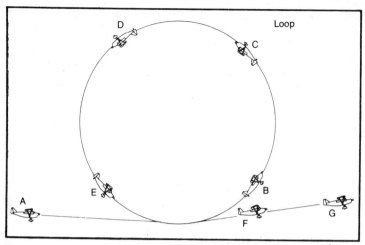

Fig. 8-4. A symmetrical loop. (A) Attain entry speed. (B) Begin pullup and start torque correction with right rudder. (C) Ease off back pressure and right rudder. (D) Increase back pressure and begin to close throttle. (E) Increase back pressure; close throttle. (F) Return to level flight.

becoming inverted, reduce your back pressure so the aircraft will overcome the effects of gravity and continue to round off the top of your loop. At this point your centrifugal force is lessening and, as your airspeed slows, gravity will try to force the loop into an unsymmetrical, egg-shaped arc (Fig. 8-5). If you lessen your back pressure as you go over the top, the loop should remain round.

After you cross inverted and start down the back side of the loop, again increase your back pressure to help round off the second half of the loop. Also at this point begin to reduce your power to idle to avoid a power dive, which would cause you to pull far more Gs in order to round off the bottom of the loop. Reducing the power will also help keep your airspeed within reasonable limits. Hopefully, you will be able to wind up the loop at the same heading, altitude and airspeed the same as you started with (Fig. 8-6).

As you return to level flight attitude, return your power to cruise and you're ready to try it again.

One of the most common problems many pilots have in completing a loop is maintaining a wings-level attitude throughout the maneuver. Part of this comes from a failure to compensate for torque and P-factor. As you know, anytime you are in a climbing situation, with power on, you have to correct for the effects of torque and P-factor. So, as you climb during the first half, add right rudder to maintain your heading and aid in keeping the wings level.

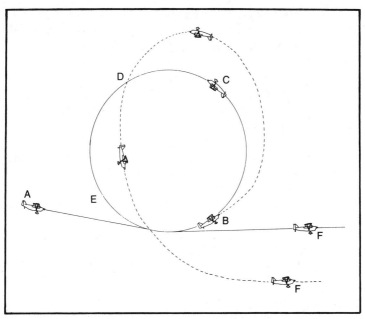

Fig. 8-5. A common loop error. If back pressure is not steadily increased from point B to C, the loop will become egg shaped as shown by the dotted line.

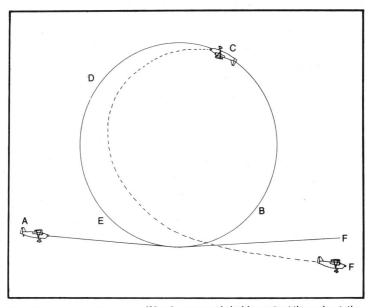

Fig. 8-6. A common loop error. If back pressure is held constant throughout, the loop will not be symmetrical as shown by the dotted line.

Then, because your aircraft is rigged to counteract torque at cruise airspeeds and cruise power settings only, you will have to add left rudder as the aircraft comes down the back side of the loop because you are accelerating without power.

Another common problem is that too many pilots fail to pull the stick *straight* back as they enter a loop. They often pull the stick toward the arm they are using to work the stick, which causes the wing on that side to drop off into a slight bank. This can cause the heading to end up different from the one on which the loop was entered. The solution, then, for most roll problems in a loop is to come *straight* back on the stick and add right rudder as you go up the front side and left rudder as you come down the back side. This will counteract the effects of torque through the first half of the loop, and the lack of the torque as the airplane accelerates without power on the back side of the loop.

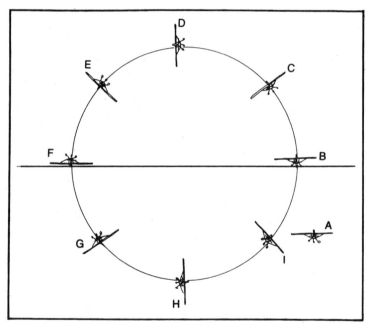

Fig. 8-7. Barrel roll. From point A to B begin pullup. From B to C continue pullup and add left aileron and left rudder. From C to D keep in full left aileron and begin easing off left rudder. From D to E continue full left aileron and begin decreasing back pressure. From E to F continue full left aileron and neutralize elevator and rudder. From F to G continue full left aileron. From G to H continue left aileron and begin to reapply left rudder and back pressure. From H to I continue full left aileron, left rudder, and back pressure to return aircraft to level flight. On return to level flight, neutralize all controls.

BARREL ROLLS

The barrel roll is one of my favorite aerobatic maneuvers. It is a smooth, fluid roll that, if executed properly, makes you feel as if you are flying your aircraft like a knife through hot butter. It is also very good in helping you learn orientation throughout a 360-degree roll while not keeping you in any one position for any length of time (Fig. 8-7). I think this type of training is invaluable to any pilot, whether you intend to continue in aerobatics or not.

To begin training on barrel rolls, get plenty of altitude and clear the airspace around, under, and over your intended practice area. Attain the manufacturer's recommended entry speed for your particular aircraft for barrel rolls. (If, for some reason, you don't know the manufacturer's recommended speed, about normal cruise plus 10 percent should work for most aircraft.) Begin a slight dive, if necessary, to attain entry speed. When you reach entry speed,

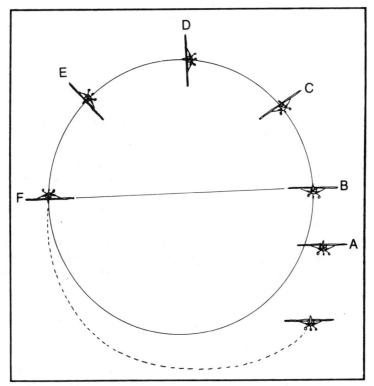

Fig. 8-8. A common barrel roll error. If the back pressure is reapplied too soon, at F, the aircraft will descend too low and destroy the symmetry of the roll as shown by the dotted line.

123

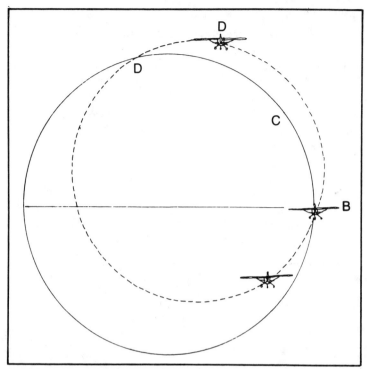

Fig. 8-9. A common barrel roll error. If the nose is pulled up too high prior to initiating the roll, the symmetry is distorted as shown by the dotted line.

initiate a smooth pull-up. As the nose crosses the horizon, continue to pull up and add coordinated aileron and rudder in the direction you wish to roll. In the beginning, I believe you will find it easier to roll to the left since you will have the effects of torque and P-factor helping the roll.

After you rotate the first 45 degrees, begin to ease off the rudder pressure but continue to apply back pressure and aileron until you arrive at the 90-degree point of the roll.

As you arrive at the 90-degree point, continue your aileron pressure, get completely off the rudder, and begin to reduce the back pressure so that when you arrive at the 180-degree point (inverted) you will have removed all the back pressure.

Continue the roll using aileron only until you arrive at the 270-degree point. Here you begin to apply back pressure and rudder once again to complete the barrel roll back to your original heading and altitude in level flight.

The list of common errors in a barrel roll is long. The one I see the most is pilots quitting before they roll 360-degrees. For some reason unknown to me many pilots reach a point about 300 degrees through the roll and just let up on all of the controls. This lets the aircraft fly away in a diving turn. I think their failure to keep their head upright has a great deal to do with the problem. This brings up a point that should be adhered to in all forms of flight: A pilot must "ride" with the aircraft. Only by keeping your head up right can you really see your attitude relative to the horizon. That goes for the rest of your body, too. Don't lean against a turn. Sit upright in your aircraft at all times and then everything will appear as it *is*, not as it should be.

When I fly with a student (aerobatic or otherwise) and he tends to lean against me, I shove him bodily back to his own space. He soon learns to sit still and his visual references become better ingrained. In our Decathlon, in which we teach aerobatics, I sit behind the student and if his head should move during a maneuver, I do not hesitate to reach up and bang him upside the head to get him back to reality. After all, your head can tilt only so far. While you can get away with a slight tilt in a small bank to make everything look level, do you think your head can make the necessary adjustments during a roll? I think not, so sit still and see things in their proper perspective. You'll be glad you did.

The other most common errors associated with a barrel roll are pictured in Figs. 8-8 and 8-9 to help you get a better idea of the symmetry—or lack thereof—and aid you in your quest for precision.

Chapter 9

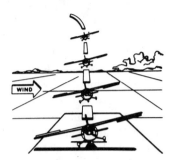

Conclusion

It is my sincere hope that if you have learned anything from this book, it is that precision is something that must be *worked* for. Few if any pilots are born with the innate quality we call precision; It must be learned by constant attention to detail and continuous striving for perfection. By always attempting to do your best, you can only get better. By feeling you are already precise, and that you are above all the rest of us mortals, your skills can only erode—which will ultimately lead to your aeronautical downfall.

Very often I witness an arrival or departure at our airport that makes me shake my head in futility. Some pilots, usually the non-precision variety, seem to believe that an uncontrolled airport is associated with non-precision pilots. Nothing could be further from the truth. In fact, at an uncontrolled field, a pilot is called upon to exercise more precision and thinking than at any other place I can think of. There is not a soul to tell you what to do and when to do it. Nobody clears you to taxi, take off, land, or anything else. You have to rely on your training, logic, and common courtesy to fly among a group of pilots and get along without bumping into each other—literally or figuratively.

Then, just as 10 or 12 precise pilots are working around the airport, along comes a B-1 (which at our airport is code for a probable businessman flying himself—or to put it another way, put your pupils to the horizon because he may come from anywhere) and he's flying a pattern that he calls "loose." We call it a "shuttle

Fig. 9-1. "So when this DC-3 got smart, I bit him."

go-around" pattern since it is so large that the space shuttle could probably execute a go-around inside this "loose" pattern.

Invariably, the B-1 will call a downwind. Good. But he's nowhere to be seen. This is because he is usually at least eight miles out—maybe on downwind and maybe not. After you search the skies (often in vain) for awhile, you decide maybe you heard wrong; it was another airport he was calling, and you go on about your business.

Then, five to seven minutes later, you hear someone call a four-mile final. Look out! He's still here. Everyone hustles to make way for the jet you're sure is on final. After you circle for several minutes, a spot appears on final. It gets larger and larger. What is it? Why, it's a Piper Lance zooming down final at 80 knots, bad-mouthing everyone in sight because *they* got in his way. After dribbling along he finally wheelbarrows it to a stop at the far end of a 5000-foot runway and then gets on the radio hot and heavy. He tells everyone on 122.8 just how incompetent they are and that they should probably seek some dual in traffic patterns and radio usage. He does this while taxiing through every puddle and over every rock on his way to the tie-down area, where he usually abandons the aircraft in a tie-down spot, leaves it untied, jumps into his sports car and departs. Thank heavens, he's finally out of the sky—now we can get back to some serious business.

Now, not all businessmen are like this, so please don't get the wrong idea. Many of them are fine pilots, but I had to use somebody.

The point I'm trying to make is that *precision shows*. Conversely, the lack thereof also shows. It stands out like a J-3 Cub at O'Hare. Precise pilots fly every type of aircraft known. They fly for the airlines, companies, charter, agriculture, flight instruction, for fun and for profit. They are to be found in all phases of aviation. Don't you want to be counted among the elite, the precise? If so, continue your practice. Seek out some good advice from some good pilots. Watch the really great pilots. Learn by example and practice. Keep practicing until you retire from aviation because only by ongoing upgrading of your skills will you be able to say without question, "I am a precise pilot. I fly with precision."

Good luck.

Index

About the Author

David A. Frazier is a former professional pilot. He heads the flight program at Vincennes University in Indiana.